Patriots, Stand Up!

This land is our land;
Fight to take it back

Russell W. Peterson

Cedar Tree Books, Ltd
Wilmington, Delaware

First Edition

Published by: **Cedar Tree Books**
9 Germay Drive, Wilmington, Delaware 19804

ISBN: 1-892142-20-1

Title: Patriots, Stand Up!
Editor: Nicholas L. Cerchio III
Copyeditor: Karen Druliner
Cover design: Sandy Hughes
Layout and book design: Phil Maggitti

Library of Congress Cataloging-in-Publication Data

Peterson, Russell W. (Russell Wilbur), 1916-
Patriots, stand up! : this land is our land, fight to take it back / Russell W. Peterson.
p. cm.
ISBN 1-892142-20-1
1. Political participation — United States.
2. United States — Politics and government — 2001-
3. United States — Foreign relations — 2001-
4. Bush, George W. (George Walker), 1946- I. Title.
JK1764.P48 2003
973.931— dc22   2003023800

Permission to use portions of this book is given freely by the author without fee for any non-commercial or educational purpose as long as proper credit is given to the author and source.

Printed in the Unites States of America

Made from recyclable materials.

Contents

Acknowledgments vii
Foreword by the Author ix
1. Integrity versus Lies and Deceit 1
2. Bush's Imperial Strategy 13
3. History's Most Powerful War Machine:
   The Military-Industrial Complex 19
4. War on the Environment31
5. Going It Alone:
   The United States versus the Rest of the World 41
6. From Love to Hate 51
7. The Bush Doctrine
   Deliberately Plunging into Debt
   And Demeaning the Needy 55
8. Using Terrorism to Frighten,
   Threaten and Exploit 65
9. A Call to Action 75

Acknowledgments

Of special importance to the production of this book was the contribution of my partner and wife June. Her encouragement, help and critique were invaluable.

All the pages of this book started out in my handwritten scrawl, but thanks to Rita McWhorter and her word processor, they were transformed into a neat manuscript.

I am especially appreciative of the work of my friend Pat Cahn, in reviewing my initial draft, and of Karen Druliner, in copyediting the final version. Thanks also to Chad Tolman for his helpful suggestions. The impressive cover was designed by Sandy Hughes.

Finally I express my gratitude to Nicholas Cerchio III and his Cedar Tree Books team for converting my manuscript on a tight deadline into an attractive book.

Foreword by the Author

Today is a frightening time for America. Far right-wing Republicans now control the White House, Senate and House of Representatives, and upon the retirement of just one Supreme Court justice, may control that body as well. This domination by extremists is the product of a "vast right-wing" conspiracy that has been growing in strength over the past few decades, using evil tactics and strategies to transform America. They have launched a full-scale attack on the way of life Americans have created over many decades through a democratic and collaborative approach. It is time for American patriots to stand up and fight to regain their cherished way of life, the envy of most of the world *until recently*.

I view this disturbing scene from the vantage point of firsthand experience, as a former Republican governor, a presidential appointee in two Republican administrations and a leader of several national and international organizations.

As an active Republican, I first saw the rise of extremism in the party when I served as a Rockefeller delegate to the 1964 Republican National Convention in San Francisco, where their candidate, Barry Goldwater, was nominated. Meeting privately with Nelson Rockefeller at the time I became aware of the stream of dirty tricks and lies being resorted to by the Goldwater supporters. On the final night of the convention, I sat in the balcony with my wife, who had been frightened the previous day by the anti-Rockefeller rage around her. Now I too found the atmosphere of hatred to be frightening. When their enemy, Nelson Rockefeller, appeared to speak, the Goldwater people around us shouted "kill him!" As Rockefeller tried to begin his speech, boos drowned him out. After an interminable period, he gave up. When Goldwater appeared, the stands erupted. Barry gave them the meat they wanted when he proclaimed their battle cry, "Extremism in the defense of liberty is no vice. Moderation in the pursuit of justice is no virtue."

Over the ensuing years as I continued to try to work as a Republican in several high-level positions, I have seen that hatred of us so-called liberals reemerge—but at no time as seriously as now. It is not only Democrats these far-right Republicans tag as liberals, but anyone who stands in their way, including moderates in their own party. "Rockefeller Republicans" are still anathema to them because Nelson Rockefeller, a long-term, highly successful Republican governor of New York, was a giant who stood in their way.

What is their way? To build an ever more powerful military; to strengthen the military-industrial complex; to cater to their financiers, the wealthy and big business; to cut taxes so as to starve Congress of funds for social programs; to operate in the red; to go-it-alone on the world scene; to relentlessly fight regulations and laws to protect the environment; to pay scant attention to the poor and disadvantaged; to pack the courts with their kind; to deliberately destroy the character of their opponents; and to lie and deceive to reach their ends.

Their way is not the American way of life I have come to know and love.

From humble beginnings as a Wisconsin boy whose family had scant resources, I worked my way through the University of Wisconsin all the way to a Ph.D. in chemistry. For twenty-six years I rose through the ranks at the DuPont Company, ending my career there as head of a research-and-development division responsible for launching new business ventures.

During those DuPont years, my extensive volunteer work and activism in civics and human rights throughout Delaware brought me to the attention of the state Republican Party leaders, who encouraged me to run for governor. When I won, the Republican-controlled legislature and I carried out some of the most progressive advances in Delaware history. Most significant was passage of legislation that prohibited any further heavy industry from being brought into Delaware's largely unspoiled coastal zone. This involved a major conflict with the U.S. Department of Commerce, the Delaware Chamber of Commerce and thirteen of the world's biggest oil and transportation companies that had been working together for ten years to plan industrialization of Delaware's coast. One of these companies, Zapata Norness, was headed by George H. W. Bush, and this conflict earned me his enmity for life. During this battle, U.S. Secretary of Commerce Maurice Stans asked me to come to Washington, where, in front of twenty-five others, he accused me of being disloyal to my country. I said, "Hell no, I'm being loyal to future generations."

In 1971 the World Wildlife Fund awarded me their Gold Medal at a black-tie dinner in New York's Waldorf Astoria. Prince Bernhard of the Netherlands, chairman of the World Wildlife Fund, said when he presented the medal, "This is the first time ever that a community worldwide has won such a battle against the oil companies." Suddenly I found myself being recognized as a national and international environmental leader. This did not set well with business and industry, including my former employer DuPont, and it became increasingly clear that my governorship would end at one term.

The day after leaving the governor's office, I began working in New York with Governor Nelson Rockefeller helping to establish a Commission on Critical Choices for Americans. Within a few months, we met with President Nixon in the Oval Office (at the height of Watergate) and received his endorsement of our project as a National Commission; the details of our meeting may be heard on the Nixon White House tapes.

My desire to become deeply involved in the national and international environmental movement continued to mount. So when I heard that Russ Train was to leave the job of chairman of the President's Council on Environmental Quality (CEQ), I went after it. Early hopes of support from the White House were dashed when George H. W. Bush, then chairman of the Republican National Committee, took a group of oil company CEOs to the White House to talk President Nixon out of nominating me. Thanks to intervention by Nelson Rockefeller and the president's new Chief of Staff, Alexander Haig, the president did nominate me to be what he called his "minister of the environment."

General Haig, Elliot Richardson, Russ Train and William Ruckelshaus, all key members of the president's team, told me he considered all environmentalists to be kooks. And the White House tapes of April 27, 1971, show that two years before he nominated me, he had told Lee Iacocca, Henry Ford Jr. and John Ehrlichman: "Environmentalists are a group of people that aren't really one damn bit interested in safety or clean air. What they are interested in is destroying the system. They're enemies of the system . . . the great life is to have it like when Indians were here." Ironically, this was the same Nixon who signed more significant environmental protections into law than any other president before or since. He must have realized that it was politically expedient for him to do so.

My presidential appointment had to be confirmed by the Senate. Prior to appearing before the Committee on Interior and Insular Affairs, I met individually with several members, including the two most senior Republicans on the committee, Paul J. Fannin of Arizona and Clifford P. Hansen of Wyoming, both former governors. Each told me that because of strong pressure from their oil industry friends they would have to give me a rough time in the hearings, but that in the end they would vote for me because, "We governors have to stick together."

The hearings lasted three days, instead of the usual one for a position such as chairman of CEQ. All six Republicans persisted in giving me, a lifelong Republican, a hard time, while all seven Democrats, including Chairman Henry "Scoop" Jackson, the father of CEQ, supported me. Ultimately the committee voted unanimously for me.

My highly talented young staff and I got much done during the next three years, despite serious obstructionism from the White House staff. This problem increased when Vice President Ford became president and appointed Dick Cheney his chief of staff. Cheney despised all environmentalists, especially me, and what we stood for. He continually tried to block my seeing the president. With the help of others, however, I managed repeatedly to get the president to invite me personally.

Cheney tried at every turn to interfere with CEQ's mandated responsibility for administering the Environmental Impact Statement (EIS), which required all executive agencies to prepare statements describing the impact their proposed actions would have on the environment. In one attempt Cheney convinced his right-wing colleague, Secretary of the Treasury William Simon, to call a meeting of the cabinet to consider what they might do to circumvent the EIS process. When I challenged Simon's authority to do so, he backed off.

On another occasion, Cheney arranged for me to be invited to a dinner meeting in Secretary of Commerce Fred Dent's office with five captains of industry: Irving Shapiro of Du Pont, Richard Gerstenberg of General Motors, John De Butts of AT & T, Reginald Jones of General Electric and Arthur Wood of Sears. The purpose of the meeting was to rehearse our presentations for the next day's televised Summit Meeting on President Ford's Whip Inflation Now program. The president was to preside.

In their presentations all five CEOs contended that environmental regulations were a principal cause of inflation. The lone voice of opposition,

I said the regulations could have no more than half of one percent impact. Immediately Congressman Gary Brown from Michigan, seated on the sidelines and presumably sent there by Cheney, piped up to say that if I were to speak the next day with this panel I would have to say what they wanted me to say. I said, "No. If I go there, I will say what I know to be true." After some contentious conversation, the secretary adjourned the meeting. The next day, a Saturday, I stuck to my message.

President Ford left the meeting before I spoke, so on Monday morning he personally called to ask me to come immediately to the Oval Office. I went, figuring I was going to be fired. When I sat down across from him, I noticed on the desk in front of him two papers with Cheney's name on them, apparently advising the president to reprimand or fire me. The president apologized for leaving the Saturday meeting before I spoke and asked me to give him my message. He asked a few questions about my statement, appeared pleased with our discussion, and walked with me to the door, placing his hand on my shoulder as we parted. Following that meeting, I never heard or read any statement by President Ford saying that environmental regulations were a cause of inflation.

Some time later, Vice President Rockefeller called, asking me as a friend to come to his office. When I arrived he was uncharacteristically agitated. He explained how President Ford had sold him on accepting the nomination for vice president by promising to give him some major assignments. "All I do now," he said, "is take orders from a bunch of kids in the White House."

Years later in 1986, speaking in a symposium at the University of California-San Diego, Cheney bragged how he had been "the sand in the gears" in blocking Rockefeller's program proposals to the president by giving an assistant the assignment of writing a letter explaining why the vice president's proposal did not fit into the president's agenda. His disloyal action was a dirty trick but bragging about it publicly was even worse.

When President Ford, a moderate conservative, decided to listen to Cheney and other right wingers and denied Rockefeller the opportunity to be his running mate in the 1976 election, he not only dealt Nelson the most serious blow in his long service as a popular Republican leader, but at the same time lost a potent campaigner, especially among independent voters.

Cheney and his cronies knew that if Gerald Ford and Nelson

Rockefeller were re-elected in 1976, Rockefeller would become a strong candidate for the presidency in 1980. Rather than have that happen, these far-right Republicans preferred to lose in 1976. After all, President Ford was not one of them.

When I met with President Ford in the Oval Office on September 1, 1976, to tell him of my decision to resign as chairman of the President's Council on Environmental Quality, he thanked me for "doing a good job" and "for standing up for the environment against considerable opposition from the others in this office." While we walked out of the office together, I wished him well in the election, then two months away. I liked President Ford. He was a decent man. Suddenly he appeared depressed. "That damn Reagan is going to make me lose the election," he stated. I believe the president was right. Ronald Reagan had opposed Ford's nomination, and Reagan and other right wingers were still bad-mouthing their Republican president. Reagan's negative impact may well have made the difference in the close race that followed.

A few months later, when Jimmy Carter brought his strong environmental convictions to the presidency and the majority of Congress was still supportive of the environmental movement, major progress was made toward protecting the air we breathe, the water we drink, the land where we grow our food, the forests and fisheries, lakes and streams, parks and refuges.

In 1978 I became director of the Congressional Office of Technology Assessment (OTA), reporting to a board of six senators and six House members, half of them Republicans and half Democrats. Our mandate was to assess the long-term impact of technological developments economically, ecologically and politically. As a result of strong encouragement by leaders of the National Academy of Science and the National Academy of Engineering, I took the job. Both groups wanted a scientist in the position, someone who would get rid of the serious politicization that had plagued the organization.

The OTA leadership had promised me the authority to hire and fire and change some of their operating rules. When I started to do so, Senator Ted Stevens, the conservative Republican from Alaska, asked me to meet with him. His chosen meeting place was a small room in the Capitol basement, where he lit into me, demanding to know who the hell I thought I was. "You report to us," he said, "we don't report to you. If you implement your plan, I will cut your budget in half." Now that was a serious threat. He was a leading Republican on the Senate Appropriation Committee. But I told him I would rather have half my budget and a credible organization than twice my budget and no credibility. Fortunately, the board supported me.

Early on, after broad consultation, my staff and I developed a priority list of the most important issues before us. Republican Senator Orrin Hatch from Utah, who had greeted me warmly as a scientist, now was outraged by what he perceived as the liberal nature of our priority list. Unknown to me, he proceeded to write a long letter listing many improprieties I allegedly had committed. He addresssed it to our board, our large advisory committee and others, but I was readily able to convince the board and advisory committee of the falsity of his accusations.

After leaving government service, I became president of the National Audubon Society, thereby fulfilling a longtime dream. I also became deeply involved on a volunteer basis with many national and international organizations: president of the International Council for Bird Protection, president and co-founder (with Ted Turner) of the Better World Society, vice president of the World Conservation Union, several assignments with the United Nations Environment Program and chairman of the Center on the Consequences of Nuclear War.

In those roles I was frequently in the halls of Congress lobbying to stop President Reagan and his fellow Republicans' all-out assault on environmental laws and regulations. Even then the commonly expressed view of most House members, such as John Dingell of Michigan, was that their Republican opposition had suddenly become downright meanspirited. I found myself increasingly repulsed by what the Republican extremists were doing, and when the Party produced its outrageously right-wing platform in 1996, that was the last straw. I became a Democrat. Now I feel at home.

Now is the time for American patriots to understand and beware of the direction in which the current leaders seek to take this country. This book is designed to warn all thinking people of the most critical threats this extremist movement poses to our American way of life.

Russ Peterson, October 2003

1

Integrity versus Lies and Deceit

The true value of a community, a nation or a business evolves from the integrity of its members, from their ability to distinguish between right and wrong and to adhere to moral principles. Integrity is learned from the teachings and examples of one's parents, teachers, associates and leaders, and from the give and take of life experiences. Integrity is protected by a society that practices justice through law.

Over the years the United States of America has benefitted from citizens of integrity who built a society that became the envy of most of the world. Now, however, as we begin the twenty-first century, America is suffering from a disastrous loss of integrity at the highest levels, in both government and business. Of special concern is the lying and deceit that currently plague our White House and Congress. The right-wing Republicans who now lead those institutions have abandoned the truth, representing as true what is known to be false and doing it so effectively that what is false is widely accepted as being true. In so doing they are seriously transforming the choice way of life Americans created over many decades.

It is time for American patriots to stand up and fight for their cherished way of life.

Extremism has been festering for years in the right wing of the Republican party, but it has grown steadily more dangerous, now infecting the party's national leadership. Some Republicans noted the existence of these extremists years ago and opposed them, but not until one of their own, David Brock, defected and described in detail in *Blinded by the Right* the inner workings and the players in that gang, that cabal, did I realize the enormity of their threat to the American way of life. Read it and learn about the extremists now working in or advising at the highest levels of our federal government, including Vice President Dick Cheney, Trent Lott, Newt Gingrich, Kenneth Starr, Tom Delay, John Ashcroft, Ted Olson, Spencer Abraham, Clarence Thomas, Bob Bork, Jerry Falwell, Pat Robertson, Grover Norquist, Paul Wolfowitz and the billionaire extremist who financed much of this movement, Richard Mellon Scaife.

Brock describes how he helped "create a highly profitable, right-wing, big lie machine that flourished in book publishing, on talk radio and on the Internet through the 1990s, gaining him standing ovations at right-wing gatherings." He relates how his best-selling book, *The Real Anita Hill,* "was almost precisely the opposite of the truth." He points out how leading conservatives including Newt Gingrich, Rush Limbaugh, Richard Mellon Scaife and Bob Tyrell "said one thing in public and did the opposite in private."

The Bush administration plays a similar game of deception. Part of their game is to label a program to appeal to the people and then do the opposite. It started with the president's campaign implying he was a moderate by calling himself a "compassionate conservative." After almost three years the compassion has yet to surface, while his right-wing conservatism flourishes. He promotes programs that downgrade environmental protection and gives them pro-environment titles—Healthy Forests, Clear Skies, Freedom Car—and describes them as helpful to the environment.

He promises "to leave no child behind" but then underfunds his education program, causing major problems for schools nationwide. He runs what have been called "Robin Hood in reverse tax policies," taking from the poor and giving to the rich. He declared, in his January 28, 2003, State of the Union address, "This tax relief is for everyone who pays income taxes," but analysis shows that 8.1 million taxpayers with lower incomes will not benefit. He says he champions civil rights and appoints judges whose records clearly show they do not support such rights.

Beware of how the members of his administration use the term "jobs." They and their business colleagues say they will create hundreds of thousands of jobs, but instead foster legislative proposals that will have little or no impact on jobs. They oppose environmental regulations that actually create jobs, claiming they will cause the loss of hundreds of thousands of jobs.

The list goes on and on, but it reached the pinnacle when the president personally, supported by all his key subordinates, misled the American people and the world community repeatedly about his reasons for going to war with Iraq. The administration began laying the groundwork for this war early on. On September 8, 2002, Vice President Dick Cheney and National Security Adviser Condoleeza Rice reported on national television that Iraq was secretly importing aluminum tubes to be used in producing weapon grade uranium; and National Security Adviser Rice warned, "We don't want the smoking gun to be a mushroom cloud." Statements like these proliferated until, in his 2003 State of the Union address, President Bush stated, "Year after year Saddam Hussein has gone to elaborate lengths, spent enormous sums, taken great risks to build and keep weapons of mass destruction."

He followed this on March 17, 2003, in a televised speech to the nation, where he said, "Intelligence gathered by this and other governments leaves no doubt that the Iraq regime continues to possess and conceal some of the most lethal weapons ever devised." This view was reinforced by Vice President Dick Cheney's assertion, "Simply stated, there is no doubt that Saddam Hussein now has weapons of mass destruction." Cheney also warned that, "One of the real concerns about [Saddam Hussein] is his biological weapons capability."

Secretary of Defense Donald Rumsfeld's declaration, "No terrorist state poses a greater or more immediate threat to our people than the regime of Saddam Hussein in Iraq," further reinforced the president's statements.

"They just don't seem concerned about the difference between what they say and what really is," wrote Independent Progressive columnist Arianna Huffington. "The best explanation I can come up with is that we are being governed by a gang of out-and-out fanatics. The defining trait of the fanatic— be it a Marxist, a fascist, or gulp, a Wolfowitz—is the utter refusal to allow anything as piddling as evidence to get in the way of an unshakable belief."

"Deception and Democracy," the lead article in the June 2003 *New Republic,* notes that, "In the summer of 2002, Vice President Cheney made several visits to the CIA's Langley headquarters, which were understood within the Agency as an attempt to pressure the low-level specialists interpreting the raw intelligence. 'That would freak people out,' said one former CIA official. 'It is supposed to be an ivory tower. And that kind of pressure would be enormous on these young guys.' "

That same month, Paul Krugman's June 3, 2003, article in *The New York Times* stated, "Suggestions that the public was manipulated into supporting an Iraq war gain credibility from the fact that misrepresentation and deception are standard operating procedure for this administration, which—to an extent never before seen in U.S. history—systematically and brazenly distorts the facts."

Here are seven reasons the Bush administration has given for going to war:

1. Iraq has weapons of mass destruction
2. It is an immediate threat to our security
3. It is linked to al Qaeda
4. It has secretly procured aluminum tubes that could be used in producing uranium
5. It has recently sought significant quantities of uranium from Niger
6. It has mobile labs for producing biological weapons
7. It has killed thousands of people with poison gas

Today all seven are known to be false.

Prior to the war, the United Nations Security Council *did try* to discover whether Saddam Hussein had weapons of mass destruction by sending its highly experienced, professional inspection team under Hans Blix back into Iraq to search, but it found no sign of any. The UN team wanted to continue searching, but U.S. leaders blocked such action. After all, they were already committed to going to war and needed to get on with their promise to protect Americans from attacks by Iraqi terrorists whose weapons, according to information supplied by British Prime Minister Tony Blair, could reach us in forty-five minutes.

When Hans Blix retired on June 30, 2003, he expressed his belief that the Iraqis *had destroyed* their weapons of mass destruction, as they contended.

The Bush administration was nasty to France, because—instead of supporting the United States—France led fellow Security Council members Russia, Germany and China in opposing a UN resolution to sanction an invasion of Iraq. I believe the Council did so because it knew the Bush administration was not telling the truth about its reasons for invading. After all, these four powerful, experienced countries do have excellent intelligence agencies of their own.

Just before the war, in a February 14, 2003, *New York Times* op-ed piece, the French Ambassador to the United States explained his country's caution about taking the offensive with Iraq: "Although we believe that the biggest threat to peace and stability is al Qaeda, we haven't seen any evidence of a direct link between the Iraq regime and al Qaeda." He pointed out that Iraq was not an immediate threat and that it would be difficult to bring democracy to a country as complex as Iraq, warning, "You can't create democracy with bombs." And finally he pointed out that "a war in Iraq could result in more frustration and bitterness in the Arab and Muslim worlds."

Both diplomatically and with regard to security, it was unwise of the Bush administration to ignore this advice and antagonize two atomic powers, France and Russia, because they didn't support the United States decision to "protect" itself from a country seven thousand miles away that had no nuclear capability. According to James Risin's June 18, 2003, column in *The New York Times*, a Defense Intelligence Agency report dated November 2002 stated that Saddam Hussein was not likely to use his weapons of mass destruction "short of an all out invasion of Iraq," or if "regime survival was imminently threatened." This supported George Tenet's earlier letter to Congress in which he wrote, "Iraq might use its weapons but only if attacked."

If anyone had any doubt about Iraq's possession of weapons of mass destruction, it should have been dispelled when the United States and Britain invaded and overwhelmed the Iraqi forces. Can you imagine a brutal dictator like Saddam Hussein, with his whole empire collapsing around him, not unleashing his most powerful weapons, his weapons of mass destruction? Certainly not, because he didn't have any. And that's why 150,000 American troops scouring Iraq haven't found any. And that's also why the warning from President Bush and his team that Iraq was an imminent threat to American security was so shamefully untrue.

The Bush team has repeatedly attempted to exploit the 9/11 terrorist attack by contending there was a link between Iraq and al Qaeda. For example the president, in his victory speech from the deck of the aircraft carrier *Abraham Lincoln,* proclaimed that with their 9/11 attacks on the United States, "the terrorists and their supporters declared war on the United States, and war is what they got." In other words, Iraq was one of those supporters so we got even.

But no one, including British intelligence, has been able to validate an Iraq-al Qaeda link. The United Nations terrorism committee, after an extensive study of Osama bin Laden's operations worldwide, found no connection with Iraq. Dafna Linzer of the Associated Press, on June 27, 2003, quoted Michael Chandler, the terrorism committee's chief investigator, as saying, "Nothing has come to our notice that would indicate links between Iraq and al Qaeda ." The first they heard of possible links was from Secretary Colin Powell when he addressed the Security Council in February 2003.

Syndicated columnist Bill Press wrote on May 31, 2003, "There is zero evidence of any link between Saddam Hussein and Osama bin Laden. No paper trail. No bank accounts. No training camps. No telephone logs. Yes, the al Qaeda network is still alive and still planning acts of terror from inside Afghanistan, Iran, Syria and Saudi Arabia. But it apparently never was inside Iraq."

It also was well known that Osama bin Laden and Saddam Hussein came from different Muslim sects and hated each other, so it is unlikely they would have helped each other. James Risin reports in *The New York Times* on June 9, 2003, that according to several intelligence officials, "Two of the highest ranking leaders of al Qaeda in American custody have told the CIA in separate interrogations that the terrorist organizations did not work jointly with the Iraqi government of Saddam Hussein." One of them told his questioners that "the idea of working with Mr. Hussein's government had been discussed among Qaeda leaders but that Osama bin Laden had rejected such proposals . . . because he didn't want to be beholden to Mr. Hussein."

In his 2003 State of the Union Address, the president also stated, "Our intelligence sources tell us that he [Saddam Hussein] has attempted to purchase high strength aluminum tubes suitable for nuclear weapons production." Soon his own Departments of State and Energy proved him wrong. The Department of Energy concluded, after consulting with its nuclear experts, that the tubes were the wrong specification to be used to enrich uranium. The State Department's Bureau of Intelligence and Research concluded that the tubes, which were openly purchased on the Internet, were to be used for a UN-approved multiple-rocket-launching system. The International Atomic Energy Agency agreed.

The president also said, "The British government has learned that Saddam Hussein recently sought significant quantities of uranium from Africa." A few days thereafter the International Atomic Energy Agency informed the world that the British story was based on forged documents. This seemed a mere mistake—until it became known that the administration was aware of the spuriousness of this scare ten months before the president delivered his speech. The best evidence comes from former Ambassador Joseph C. Wilson IV in the July 6, 2003, *The New York Times*. He had served for twenty-three years as a career foreign service officer and ambassador, and had worked in Iraq and Niger, the two countries allegedly involved in the uranium ore purchase. Wilson reports how, in February 2002, he was told by the Central Intelligence Agency that it had been asked by Vice President Cheney's office to check out an intelligence report on the Niger to Iraq issue. The CIA asked Wilson to travel to Niger to do so. He concluded it was extremely doubtful that the alleged transaction occurred, and Niger formally denied the charge. Wilson provided detailed briefing to both the CIA and the State Department's African Affairs Bureau. The CIA reported back to the vice president.

In view of all the information showing the Niger to Iraq postulation phony, someone needs to explain how it got into the president's speech. Was it a slipup or the work of one of the hawks around the president? Wilson said in a *Washington Post* interview, "It really comes down to the administration misrepresenting the facts on an issue that was a fundamental justification for going to war. It begs the question, what else are they lying about?"

What better place to learn of the integrity (or lack thereof) of the Bush administration on intelligence matters than the intelligence community itself? These proud professionals are so embittered by the way their work has been grossly distorted and manipulated by the war hawks running our country that many are now coming forth to say so. Nicholas D. Kristof, in his June 1, 2003, column in *The New York Times* reports, "The outrage among the intelligence professionals is so widespread that they have formed a group, Veteran Intelligence Professionals for Sanity, that wrote to President Bush this month to protest what it called 'a policy and intelligence fiasco of monumental proportions.'" Kristof further notes that, "While there have been occasions in the past when intelligence has been deliberately warped for political purposes ...never before has such warping been used in such a systematic way to mislead our elected representatives into voting to launch a war." The political advantage such deceit has gained for our leaders so far is frightening indeed.

The United States claim that Iraq has mobile facilities for producing biological weapons also is highly questionable. The idea of using such facilities was explored many years ago by the U.S. military as a backup for germ warfare manufacturing plants it was operating. Presumably the United States terminated all such activities when we signed the 1975 global treaty banning the use of bio-weapons.

In 1999 an Iraqi engineer who had defected told U.S. officials that he had been involved with a mobile bio-weapon plant. Shortly thereafter, according to a July 2, 2003, *New York Times* story, the United States constructed a mobile plant to train Special Operations Units. It was "real in all its parts but never actually plugged in," they said. This background led U.S. leaders to speculate that Iraq had such mobile units. So when our troops found two mobile labs in Iraq that might have been used for a part of a germ-manufacturing process, our leaders called them a "smoking gun." No evidence has been found to indicate the trailers were ever used to make a biological weapon precursor.

Director of Central Intelligence George Tenet, however, concluded that the trailers were meant for that purpose. The State Department's intelligence bureau sent a classified document to Secretary Powell on June 2, 2003, questioning Tenet's appraisal and suggesting that a possible intended use of the trailers was for refueling anti-aircraft missiles. Nevertheless, President Bush, Prime Minister Tony Blair and Secretary of State Colin Powell have continued to use these trailers as support for their claim that weapons of mass destruction have been found. Iraqis, however, have shown United Nations inspectors many photographs and videos of the variety of purposes for which Iraq has been using such mobile units. Regardless of the use for which these sterile trailers might have been intended, it is hard to envision how anyone could honestly claim that they had found in them the weapons for which they were searching.

James Dao and Thom Shanker reported in *The New York Times* on May 30, 2003, that Lt. Gen. James Conway, Commander of the First Marine Expeditionary Force in Iraq, told reporters that he was amazed that Iraq did not fire biological or chemical weapons on the American forces marching toward Baghdad. They quote Conway as saying, "It was a surprise to me then, it remains a surprise to me now, that we have not uncovered [such] weapons in some of the forward dispersal sites. Again, believe me, it's not for lack of trying. . . . What the regime was intending to do in terms of its use of the weapons, we thought we understood. We were simply wrong."

Five of Saddam Hussein's most prominent scientists, who had been involved in Iraq's earlier work with bio-weapons, have been in U.S. custody for months, undergoing intense interrogation. They have been promised safe haven outside Iraq. All five separately and repeatedly testified that Iraq had destroyed its banned weapons after the Gulf War when the Security Council so ordered and has never resumed production. This explains the failure of the United Nations inspectors and the United States and British military to find any.

A further example of misinformation used by the White House in the buildup to war was that Saddam Hussein was responsible for killing thousands of his own citizens with poison gas at Halabja in northern Iraq. Stephen C. Pelletiere, in an op-ed piece in *The New York Times* on January 31, 2003, throws a different light on this. He explains that he was the senior political analyst on Iraq for the Central Intelligence Agency during the eight-year war between Iran and Iraq, served as a professor at the Army War College from 1988-2000 and headed a 1991 Army investigation into how the Iraqis would conduct a war against the United States Both this investigation and one by the U.S. Defense Intelligence Agency immediately after the Iran-Iraq war reported in depth on the Halabja affair. Both reports are in the U.S. intelligence community's files.

In 1988 Iran captured Halabja, a Kurdish site just inside the Iraqi border and one which commands the major source of water for the Persian Gulf states. Iraq counterattacked. Both sides used gas—Iraq a mustard gas and Iran a cyanide-based gas, the latter a much more deadly agent. But, as Pelletiere writes, "The condition of the dead Kurds' bodies, however, indicated they had been killed with a blood agent—that is, a cyanide-based gas—which Iran was known to use. The Iraqis, who are thought to have used mustard gas in the battle, are not known to have possessed blood agents at the time."

Pelletiere goes on to state, "I am not trying to rehabilitate the character of Saddam Hussein. He has much to answer for in the area of human-rights abuses. But accusing him of gassing his own people at Halabja as an act of genocide is not correct, because as far as the information we have goes, all of the cases where gas was used involved battles. These were tragedies of war. There may be justification for the United States to invade Iraq, but Halabja is not one of them."

Despite being aware of this information, the Bush administration continued to misrepresent what occurred at Halabja as part of the planned build-up to war. In consequence of this and other known falsifications, America's most trustworthy and creditable newspaper, *The New York Times*, editorialized on June 8, 2003, "If the intelligence is wrong, or the government distorts it, the United States will squander its credibility. Even worse, it will lose the ability to rally the world, and the American people, to the defense of the country when real threats materialize." To this I add my own opinion that such consequences would be even more serious than removing a sitting president.

Few people are better informed on that subject than former White House counsel John Dean, who blew the whistle on President Nixon. Robert Scheer in the June 20, 2003, *Los Angeles Times* quoted John Dean's June 6 contribution to the Web site Federal Law: "To put it bluntly, if Bush has taken Congress and the nation into war based on bogus information, he is cooked. Manipulation or deliberate misuse of national security intelligence data, if proven, could be a 'high crime' under the Constitution's impeachment clause. It would also be a violation of federal criminal law, including the broad federal anti-conspiracy statute, which renders it a felony 'to defraud the United States or any agency thereof in any manner or for any purpose.' "

Now that it is obvious that the Bush administration leadership has deceived us into war, what are we, the American people, going to do about it?

Disturbingly, most of our political leaders are doing nothing about it. Paul Krugman's, June 24, 2003, *New York Times* column said this is "because they don't want to face the implications. If you admit to yourself that such a thing happened, you have a moral obligation to demand accountability—and to do so in the face not only of a powerful, ruthless political machine but in the face of a country not yet ready to believe that its leaders have exploited 9/11 for political gain, it's a scary prospect.

"Yet if we can't find people willing to take the risk—to face the truth and act on it—what will happen to our democracy?" Shouldn't the American people and the world community demand that those guilty of this deception be held accountable?

The principal architect of the deceit that is a hallmark of the Bush administration is fifty-three-year-old Karl Rove. He has practiced this evil trait all his professional life, even taught it as a professor at the University of Texas. He excels at it. His greatest accomplishment in using it was his transformation of an ill-equipped, perennial failure and fellow Texan into governor of Texas, then president of the United States and leader of the free world. Rove's skill is not in promoting his candidate, but in tearing down the opposition with a barrage of outrageous falsifications. His tactic, a serious affront to democracy, has made him feared and admired by Republicans and Democrats alike. His unprincipled but successful approach has led to his becoming the primary adviser to the president and the president's men and women on a wide variety of issues. Some say that the president is so indebted to Rove that his ears are wide open to Rove's whisperings. In any case, he is one of the big five at the head of our government who practice the Rove technique: the president, Rove himself, Vice President Cheney, Secretary of Defense Rumsfeld and National Security Adviser Rice. Secretary of State Powell is also a powerhouse, but he is not one of them. I wonder why he stays there.

If you would like an in-depth, firsthand review of the Machiavellian methods that brought Rove to the pinnacle of power, read *Bush's Brain: How Karl Rove Made George W. Bush Presidential.* The authors, James Moore and Wayne Slater, two journalists who have served Texas and national politics for years, traveled extensively on George W. Bush's gubernatorial and presidential campaigns and watched Karl Rove in action. One incident they relate describes well the Bush-Rove team at work. In the 2000 South Carolina primary battle between George Bush and John McCain, who had just walloped Bush in New Hampshire, Bush repeatedly proclaimed his determination to observe high campaign standards. But his people "leveled a savage direct-mail and phone campaign against" the war hero John McCain and even questioned his loyalty. When McCain challenged him, Bush reached over to grasp his rival's hand and said the two should put their acrimony behind them. "Don't give me that shit," said McCain, "and take your hands off me."

Negative campaigning has been with us ever since Colonial days, but it has never been practiced so skillfully, extensively and brutally as by Karl Rove—nor has it ever before had so many tens of millions of dollars to use in spewing its evil through the news media. The time has come to blow the whistle—to hold accountable both Karl Rove and those who clearly hold office because of him.

After the president, in his 2003 State of the Union message, proclaimed to the world the now well-known forgery about Iraq ordering uranium from Niger, a well-established string of mea culpas sounded from his team—first from CIA Director George Tenet, then from Deputy National Security Adviser Stephen Hadley and then from Hadley's boss, Condoleeza Rice. Finally the anchor man for this relay to the top, the president himself, said in a nationally televised press conference, "I take personal responsibility for everything I say." You bet he does. And we will hold him to it, even when it's written by Karl Rove.

Fellow patriots, I ask you to recall the inspiring words of Thomas Jefferson, inscribed for all to see in his memorial in our nation's capital: "I have sworn upon the altar of God eternal hostility against every form of tyranny over the mind of man." Our current leaders should give serious consideration to these words.

2

Bush's Imperial Strategy

The so-called National Security Strategy created by the Bush administration in September 2002 is a major threat to the American way of life. It calls for the United States to intervene unilaterally and preemptively in countries judged to be a threat to America. It sees our overwhelmingly dominant military power as the means to that end.

According to the National Security Strategy, "The United States can no longer rely on a reactive posture as we have in the past. The inability to deter a potential attacker, the immediacy of today's threats and the magnitude of potential harm that could be caused by our adversaries' choice of weapons, do not permit that option. We cannot let our enemies strike first." In other words the United States could strike without garnering the approval of any other body including the United Nations, even though the United Nations Charter requires its approval.

The Bush strategy evolved from the work over the previous two decades of a small group of young, radical, right-wing Republican intellectuals. Most prominent among them were Paul Wolfowitz and Richard Perle, who brought their hard-line militarism to bear on the Department of Defense during the Reagan and senior Bush administrations. For example, in 1992 Wolfowitz, as under secretary of defense for policy reporting to Secretary Cheney, drafted a Defense Policy Guidance paper calling for a preemptive strike against Iraq.

The plans of this militaristic group, although relegated to the back burner during the Clinton years, continued to simmer. They established a think tank called the Project for the New American Century that included Paul Wolfowitz, I. Lewis Libby and two former secretaries of defense, Donald Rumsfeld and Dick Cheney. In September 2000 (two months before George W. Bush's election), they published a report entitled "Rebuilding America's Defenses: Strategies, Forces and Resources for a New Century."

When George W. Bush became president and Dick Cheney vice president, they brought into their circle a substantial number of members of this think tank, including I. Lewis Libby as chief of staff for Cheney, Donald Rumsfeld as secretary of defense, Paul Wolfowitz as his chief of staff and Wolfowitz's buddies, Douglas Firth, William Luti and Abram Shulsky, as key assistants. So it was not surprising when the Bush administration's National Security Strategy subsequently appeared, that it closely followed the recommendations of the September 2000 report "Rebuilding America's Defenses."

The first application of the Bush strategy came with the 2003 attack on Iraq. In its efforts to justify the attack, the Bush administration concocted several faulty examples of an Iraqi threat to America. Its efforts were enhanced by telling the American people that Saddam Hussein was involved in the tragic September 11, 2001, terrorist attack on the World Trade Center and the Pentagon. Although no evidence of this was ever uncovered, a February 2003 poll showed that 72 percent of Americans believed it.

When the United States and other intelligence agencies began to question the reality of the threats articulated by the president and others, Rumsfeld and Wolfowitz established an Office of Special Plans to get the evidence they wanted, especially that Iraq and al Qaeda were working together. As reported by Seymour M. Hersh in *The New Yorker*, May 12, 2003, Wolfowitz selected Abram Shulsky as director of the office. The two had graduated together from the University of Chicago with Ph.D.s in 1972. Shulsky had worked under Richard Perle, assistant secretary of defense during the Reagan administration. Under Secretary of Defense William Luti, another hard liner, was assigned by Wolfowitz to oversee the office of special plans. The eighteen members of this group called themselves "The Cabal."

Seymour Hersh quoted a Pentagon adviser who had worked with Special Operations, "Shulsky and Luti won the debate. They cleaned up on State and the CIA ... [and] persuaded the president of the need to make a new security policy." And when Secretary of State Colin Powell failed to convince the United Nations Security Council to support a U.S. attack on Iraq, the United States and its ally, Britain, went ahead pre-emptively.

When asked why the United States had picked Iraq as its first target rather than Syria or Iran, Wolfowitz said, "Iraq was the easiest." After all it was almost defenseless. The earlier war with the United States, United Nations sanctions and disarmament enforced by UN inspectors had made it so. It had no significant weaponry—and certainly no weapons of mass destruction.

With over twenty thousand sorties by aircraft facing no opposition, with precision guided missiles launched from ships hundreds of miles away, with over 150,000 armor-clad ground troops supported by impenetrable tanks and super fire-power, the United States and British team wiped out the lightly clad and ill-equipped Iraqi opposition in short order. Fewer than two hundred U.S. and British military died in the official war. A large, but strangely unannounced number of Iraqi military died, along with an estimated five to seven thousand Iraqi civilians.

If anyone needed convincing that America was *the* military superpower, the sophisticated, highly technological, awesome demonstration of our military in action should have done so. Yes, wiping out the brutal, inhumane regime of Saddam Hussein was a major and desirable accomplishment. But it was—and still is—wrong for the Bush administration to proclaim that getting rid of Saddam Hussein was adequate justification for the war. The falsifications they used to con the Congress and the American people into supporting the war will forever tarnish the victory, as will the fact that they chose to "go it alone," rather than working with the United Nations.

As we look to the future it is important to recognize that America's unilateral imperial strategy may be all about oil, about using its military might to gain control of the world's petroleum resources. Such policy could be a direct result of the growing realization among oil companies that world production of oil will peak within a few years and then start its long descent toward zero. The former oil and energy company executives now running our country, including President Bush and Vice President Cheney, know well that is what happened in the lower forty-eight states in 1970. No matter how many new wells they drilled after that, the total production went down. President Bush learned that firsthand when his own Texas oil company failed to find significant amounts of oil.

The famous petroleum scientist, King Hubbert, predicted accurately in 1948 that production in the lower forty-eight would peak about 1970. Furthermore, he calculated that the world peak would come in the first few years of the twenty-first century, and when that happened, oil prices would soar. The United States was well endowed with oil in places like Texas and Oklahoma, but we pumped it out rapidly, even becoming oil exporters. Since then, while our consumption of oil has skyrocketed, we have become increasingly dependent on others—especially the Middle Eastern countries, which have the largest remaining oil reserves.

Our invasion of Iraq opens the door to the country considered by many oil-company experts as "the biggest hope in the oil world." What's more, it gives the United States a place at the table with other big Mideast producers—Saudi Arabia, Iran, Kuwait, United Arab Emirates and Syria. Imagine the enthusiasm today in the board rooms of U.S. oil companies like Exxon-Mobil, the oil-dependent auto companies like General Motors, and the energy conglomerates like Halliburton (whose recent CEO was Vice President Dick Cheney). As head of President Bush's secretive task force to review U.S. energy policy, Cheney should be pleased with our occupation of Iraq, because the centerpiece of his task force proposal was to increase the production and use of fossil fuels like oil.

An article, "Beneath the Sand," by John Cassidy in the July 14 and 21, 2003, *New Yorker* throws much light on this. Cassidy reports how the Cheney task force issued a report in May 2001 that identified a "fundamental imbalance between supply and demand" as the core of "our nation's energy crisis." He notes that, "We produce 39 percent less oil today than we did in 1970, leaving us ever more reliant on foreign suppliers. On our present course, America 20 years from now will import two out of every thee barrels of oil—a condition of increased dependency on foreign powers that does not always have America's interests at heart."

Cassidy continued, "In a less publicized passage, it called on the Bush administration to make 'energy security a priority of our trade and foreign policy' and to encourage Middle Eastern countries to open up their energy sectors to foreign investment!" He also reports that in Nashville on August 26, 2002, Cheney warned a group of veterans that if Saddam Hussein got his hands on weapons of terror he "would seek domination of the entire Middle East" and "take control of a great portion of the world's energy supplies."

This article goes on to say, "Cheney's speech was one of the last occasions on which the Bush administration publicly acknowledged the link between energy policy and national security. Thereafter it adopted the line that the decision to remove Saddam Hussein from power had, in the words of Defense Secretary Donald Rumsfeld, 'nothing to do with oil, literally nothing to do with oil.' "

You have to be naive to believe that. Their interest in gaining control of Iraq's oil might explain why our leaders were so anxious to act unilaterally in Iraq, to keep the United Nations out of it.

The administration has also locked out environmental leaders who have been deeply concerned about the development and use of energy—principal causes of the degradation of our air, water, land and health. So, when Vice President Cheney included no environmental leaders on his task force, they were disturbed, especially when they learned the task force was dominated by oil and auto company executives and their associates. The vice president's refusal to release the names of any members added to these concerns. The Natural Resources Defense council sued to gain access to the list, and just recently a federal court ordered Vice President Cheney to produce it.

Immediately after the war was over, our government granted its first large contract for rehabilitating Iraq, specifically for restoring Iraq's devastated oil production and shipment facilities. It went without a bid to Kellogg Brown and Root, a subsidiary of Halliburton. At the same time Philip J. Carroll, a Texas oilman, was appointed as an adviser to the Iraqi Ministry of Oil. Carroll is a former senior executive at Royal Dutch/Shell. As John Cassidy reported in *The New Yorker* article cited earlier, Carroll subsequently said that "talks with foreign oil companies will probably begin before the end of this year, and that all the major Western firms, including Exxon-Mobil, Chevron, Texaco, Royal Dutch/Shell and British Petroleum would probably take part."

A comprehensive article by Richard Heinberg entitled *The End of the Oil Age*, which appeared in the Autumn 2003 *Earth Island Journal*, throws much light on the seriousness of the monumental oil crisis rapidly approaching us. He claims that the great mania of the oil companies to merge a few years ago was a scaling down of a dying industry in recognition that 90 percent of global conventional oil has already been found. Heinberg cites a lecture by energy executive Matthew Simmons in June 2001 to the American Association of Petroleum Geologists in which Simmons said, "Even the Middle East is now beginning to experience for the first time ever, how hard it is to grow production once giant oil fields roll over and begin to decline. . . . There is growing evidence that almost every giant field in the Middle East has already passed its peak production."

The most incriminating evidence that President Bush is in bed with American oil companies appeared on May 22, 2003, in his Executive Order 13303, which makes U.S. oil companies exclusively immune from any legal action in the United States involving Iraqi oil. Jim Valletti of the Institute for Policy Studies has written, "Bush's order unilaterally declares Iraq oil to be the unassailable province of U.S. corporations. . . . It is yet another Bush effort on behalf of U.S. corporations to seize control of Iraq's oil. . . . It has no basis in law or morality."

The Bush administration's imperial strategy is bad for America and the rest of the world. American patriots must stand up and change it.

3

History's Most Powerful War Machine: The Military-Industrial Complex

Under the current Bush administration, billions of borrowed dollars are being poured into the further build-up of history's most powerful war machine, placing its management under noted war hawks who lie and deceive, allowing them to override America's intelligence gathering agencies, and devising a new official strategy for using our military to dictate unilaterally to other countries. This all bodes ill for peace in America and the world. Today achieving peace is more dependent upon restoring America's damaged credibility than on its military might.

Just how big is our war machine? According to the Center for Defense Information's *Defense Monitor* (April/May 2003), America's $399 billion proposed military spending for 2004 exceeds that of the next twenty nations together, and when added to what our allies spend, is fifty-two times higher than that of the seven rogue states (Cuba, Iraq, Iran, Libya, Syria, North Korea and Sudan), countries identified by the Pentagon as our most likely adversaries. The U.S. Fiscal Year 2004 Discretionary Budget shows that defense is by far our most expensive activity—seven times that of the next highest, education. And this doesn't include the huge costs we are now experiencing in cleaning up and rebuilding Iraq.

Although we are far ahead of any other nation in the sophistication and effectiveness of our military, we continue to pour billions into ever more weapons. In fiscal year 2004 our military is scheduled to spend $9.8 billion on a highly controversial Ballistic Missile Defense system whose viability has never been demonstrated. This is a make-work project, a sop, for the powerful but struggling aerospace industry. The United States is able to do this because the Bush administration abandoned the Anti-Ballistic Missile Treaty which prohibited such action.

A major reason for this continued buildup is the military-industrial complex, which flourishes now more than ever before. President Eisenhower in his January 17, 1961, farewell address warned us to beware the military-industrial complex. After being a five-star general, commander of all Allied forces in Europe during World War II and president for eight years, he had many opportunities to observe the military-industrial complex. Here is what he said:

> We have been compelled to create a permanent armaments industry of vast proportions. Added to this, three and a half million men and women are directly engaged in the defense establishment. We annually spend on military security more than the net income of all United States Corporations.
>
> This conjunction of an immense military establishment and a large arms industry is new in the American experience. The total influence—economic, political, even spiritual—is felt in every city, every state house, every office of the Federal government. We recognize the imperative need for this development. Yet we must not fail to comprehend its grave implications. Our toil, resources and livelihood are all involved; so is the very structure of our society.
>
> In the councils of government, we must guard against the acquisition of unwarranted influence, whether sought or unsought, by the military-industrial complex. The potential for the disastrous rise of misplaced power exists and will persist.

Eisenhower's admonition still rings true. Every federal official should be required to read it before taking the oath of office.

In the June 22, 2003, issue of *The New York Times Magazine* Dan Baum provides an in-depth description of the military-industrial complex already at work in Iraq. Bechtel and Kellogg Brown & Root (KBR) have been signed up by the military to operate two of the biggest reconstruction projects now underway in Iraq. Both companies have a number of former senior U.S. government officials on their boards and staffs—people who capitalize on their knowledge and continuing influence in Washington.

Baum reports how KBR was hired to write "the Army's classified contingency plan for repairing Iraq's infrastructure" and later was hired to implement it on a cost-plus basis. This means "KBR spends whatever it believes necessary to get the job done, then adds from one to nine percent for profit." Dick Cheney first hired Brown & Root, a subsidiary of Halliburton, when he was secretary of defense in George H. W. Bush's administration. He later became Halliburton's CEO, effectively opening doors to the military during the Clinton administration. Now, as vice president, he keeps those doors open.

Bob Herbert's column in *The New York Times*, on May 22, 2003, describes Halliburton and its work with Bush's axis of evil, and ends with, "Halliburton and its subsidiaries are virtuosos at gaming the system. . . . It benefits from doing business with the enemy, from its relationship with the U.S. military when it's at war with the enemy and from its contracts to help rebuild the defeated enemy."

According to the Center for Public Integrity, the thirty members of the influential Defense Policy Board include nine current leaders of companies that got $76 billion in defense contracts in 2001 and 2002. Probably the most disreputable practitioner of this insider dealing is the cold warrior Richard Perle, who, thanks to Secretary Rumsfeld, served as chairman of the Defense Policy Board until recently when his questionable dealings caused his removal. Nevertheless he was kept on the board where he continues to operate. He is a far-right hawk who has served as assistant secretary of defense in the Reagan administration, is a strong ally of current Deputy Secretary of Defense Paul Wolfowitz and served with the far-right think tanks, American Enterprise Institute and the Project for the New American Century, in helping to define the Bush administration's foreign and military policies.

Baum writes, "It's a relatively small club that has both guided U.S. military, energy and Middle Eastern policies over the past three decades and then run the corporations that benefit from those policies. And it's a club that had a long history with Saddam Hussein." Donald Rumsfeld was the person who negotiated with Saddam Hussein in the 1980s. It has also been suggested that U.S. companies supplied Iraq with poison gas and helped it start a biological weapons program during the eight-year war with Iran.

Gore Vidal, author of *Perpetual Peace Through Perpetual War*, wrote a letter to President-elect George W. Bush dated January 11, 2001, in which he observed: "Your first big job will be to curb the Pentagon warlords and their fellow conspirators in Congress and the boardrooms of corporate America." To date this has not been done.

The costs in the aftermath of President George W. Bush's two wars in two years—Iraq and Afghanistan—are huge and growing. The bill for just supporting ongoing military operations is about $1 billion per month in Afghanistan and $4 billion per month in Iraq, or $60 billion per year for both. The costs of reconstructing these devastated countries will be much greater. The UN has estimated it will cost $19 billion for Afghanistan alone. The U.S. Congress did authorize a four-year expenditure of $2.3 billion for Afghan reconstruction, but had appropriated nothing as of September 1, 2003.

The costs of rebuilding Iraq will be markedly greater, but our government has yet to forecast an amount. In his speech to the nation on September 7, 2003, President Bush asked Congress for $87 billion for the next installment for operations in Iraq and Afghanistan and pleaded for help from the United Nations. His government is in a deep financial bind. It is broke. Thanks in great measure to the Republican mania for cutting taxes, our government is running huge deficits, borrowing more and more to pay its way. So the only recourse our leaders have for covering the huge ongoing costs of the two wars is borrowing more. Perhaps the Bush administration's alienated friends in the UN will come to his rescue. Meanwhile the futures of Afghanistan and Iraq remain unclear. Outside Kabul, Afghanistan is under the autocratic rule of aggressive regional war lords, who further guerilla warfare and the harsh treatment of women. In Iraq, guerilla warfare continues to kill and wound Americans and sabotage vital infrastructure. By September 1, 2003, more Americans had been killed or wounded in Iraq since President Bush declared the war was over in May than were lost during the war itself. And nearly every day more are lost.

Getting rid of Saddam Hussein and his gang and routing the Taliban in Afghanistan were major accomplishments, but how long it will take to bring liberty, freedom and democracy to these tortured peoples is anyone's guess. President Bush has said, "A free Iraq will mean a peaceful world." He obviously forgot the dozens of other countries now at war, many ruled by dictators who oppress their people. Oh, how those people must wish for a peaceful world!

Of all the threats the world suffers, no other comes close to nuclear weapons. As the creator of this weapon of mass destruction and the only country to ever use it in warfare, the United States has a special obligation to harness it. You have only to visit, as I did, the memorial in the center of Hiroshima where the *Enola Gay* dropped the first nuclear bomb. It made me shudder to reflect on how one bomb could obliterate so much of a good-sized city, killing approximately 120,000 civilians. And that was a minor bomb compared to the thousands now on standby in the U.S. military arsenal. From twenty-five to thirty thousand of these are targeted to fly on short notice from silos in America or from aircraft carriers or submarines at sea. They are poised on the noses of intercontinental missiles to land with high precision on preselected cities around the world.

Anyone who doubts this should read what Dr. Bruce G. Blair, president of the Center for Defense Information and former nuclear launch officer, had to say in the April/May 2003 issue of *The Defense Monitor.*

As a Minuteman missile launch officer during the 1970's, I "fought" about 100 nuclear wars in mock underground launch centers in California and Montana. . . . We read an eight-digit code from the launch order and dialed it into a panel near my chair. This code unlocks the missiles and enables them to receive the next and last computer instructions from me and my crewmate—the "fire" signal that ignites the motors and propels the missiles half way around the planet in 30 minutes. No more than two minutes elapsed between the time of the launch order's arrival and our final key-turns. . . . Launch officers in their early twenties, like myself, rarely struggled with the moral question of following orders that potentially could kill so many innocent civilians. . . . This has not changed over the decades of nuclear vigil maintained in launch centers. I have returned on occasion, most recently last year, to the great plains of the country to discuss launch duties with freshly minted crew members. . . . The strongest emotion was, and still is, the feeling of satisfaction and crew camaraderie for having pushed the right buttons at the right time in a simulated nuclear war. Perhaps more profound questions would weigh on the hearts and minds of the young men and women manning the consoles if the fateful order someday comes. . . . The thought that my son, or daughter even, might someday be expected to stand ready to fire nuclear missiles fills me with revulsion at our failed leadership in the world. It would not be his or her fault that we, as a nation, having suspended our morality during the Cold War, lacked the vision and sensibility to stand down now that it's over.

Russia ranks second to the United States in the possession of thousands of nuclear weapons and missiles to launch them. No doubt some of them are reciprocally targeted on America. Upon dissolution of the Soviet Union after the Cold War, Russia inherited the Soviet's nuclear arsenal, and along with it a myriad of problems—safeguarding the weapons, preventing an accidental launch, meaningfully employing nuclear scientists and engineers who lost their jobs in downsizing the program and funding of agreed-upon disarmament measures. The United States has provided some funding to help with this program, but now the right-wing Republican leadership of the Congress, woefully short of funds, is questioning whether to continue doing so.

The United Kingdom and France are the other two members of the foursome who possess an appreciable number of nuclear weapons and the missiles to deliver them thousands of miles away. Some nations—China, India, Pakistan, Israel and North Korea—have one or more nuclear bombs but as yet no missiles to deliver them long distances. Other nations at war with neighbors or concerned about security see membership in the nuclear club as desirable.

The anti-ballistic missile (ABM) treaty ratified by the United States in 1972 was considered a milestone in the world's attempt to reduce the competition for ever-larger nuclear arsenals. But now the Bush administration has seen fit to withdraw from that treaty, to the irritation of Russia, and to resume Ronald Reagan's Star Wars dream of building a visionary nuclear shield over America. And Congress has provided startup funds for this project which may cost as much as a trillion dollars.

It is worthwhile here to stop for a moment and recall the major effort during the 1980s to study the long-term biological consequences of a nuclear exchange between the United States and the Soviet Union. At that time, I accepted the chairmanship of the Center on Consequences of Nuclear War. We signed up Carl Sagan, a physical scientist, and Paul Ehrlich, a biologist, to lead a large group of scientists in studying the issue. The project included close liaison with Soviet scientists and culminated in a live interactive TV hookup between Moscow and Washington. The two sides showed remarkable equanimity.

Out of this work came the concept of *nuclear winter,* potentially stemming from the burning cities and forests of the world, which would emit immense clouds of smoke so dense as to block out sunlight, darken the earth and freeze substantial areas. This led to major concern and discussions worldwide, except within the Reagan administration. The work we did resulted in a book, *The Cold and the Dark*, authored by Carl Sagan, Paul Ehrlich and other scientists. Subsequent modeling calculations indicated that nuclear winter was only a remote probability. Nevertheless, a nuclear exchange would have a devastating impact on climate and biological activity. With the end of the Cold War, this concern vanished from everyone's radar screen. As the spectre of nuclear warfare now reappears, it is time to revisit that study.

In the Spring 2003 Newsletter of The Ploughshares Fund, Executive Director Naila Bolus discusses this issue. The Ploughshares Fund, for which I was an adviser, was founded in 1981 "to prevent the spread and use of nuclear, chemical, biological and other weapons of war, and to prevent conflicts that could lead to the use of weapons of mass destruction." Mr. Bolus writes that "the drastic changes in U.S. nuclear doctrine outlined by the Bush administration in last year's *Nuclear Posture Review* and later in its *National Security Strategy*, will dramatically increase the likelihood that such weapons will be used and will encourage more and more countries to acquire their own nuclear arsenals." The new doctrine even foresees, unbelievably, the use of nuclear weapons to deter the use of biological and chemical weapons.

Of special concern is the Defense Department's move to abandon the "ten-year-old ban on the research and production of nuclear weapons having the explosive force of less than five kilotons of TNT or one-third the power of the atomic bomb dropped on Hiroshima." Proponents of the mini-nukes, according to Bolus, contend that smaller nuclear weapons would be more usable and "would persuade adversaries that we would use them and thus would provide a more effective deterrent." On the contrary, it seems to me that since mini-nukes would require less explosive-grade plutonium or uranium, the U.S. program would teach and encourage small nations and especially terrorist groups to build and use them.

Another disturbing plan of the U.S. Defense Department is to forego the 1992 moratorium on the testing of nuclear weapons, a move the Pentagon contends is necessary to advance its research on new weapons. The Council for a Livable World, founded in 1962 by top nuclear scientists from leading universities to oppose weapons of mass destruction, has launched a major effort to fight the Bush administration's nuclear policies, which they characterize as "the most extreme in American history."

The Center for Arms Control and Non-Proliferation, made up of several Nobel Laureates and top professors from leading universities, reported in June 2003: "Since the 9/11 tragedy the Bush administration has pursued an unprecedented peace time military buildup, most of it unrelated to terrorism, and embraced policies of preemptive war and regime change, claiming that we are in an endless war on terrorism. . . . In fact, President Bush has abandoned arms control and is pursuing new policies that are making the world more unstable."

Especially disturbing is the well documented fact that the hawks in our Department of Defense seriously considered the use of nuclear weapons in the war on Iraq. Such legitimization of their use would surely make the world more dangerous than ever. In the May 4, 2003, issue of *The New York Times Magazine* Bill Keller's article, "The Thinkable," stated:

> During the last years of the cold war, weapons of mass destruction were mostly abstractions to be counted and negotiated. Suddenly with too few people paying attention, they are proliferating, and those who now have or want nukes will use them to blackmail, or worse.
>
> A new arms-control regime should distinguish among threats and offer a menu of options appropriate to the danger, from inspection to coercion. . . . And it would accept the solemn responsibility—a particular American responsibility—to restore the special stigma of nuclear explosives.
>
> The destructive power of these weapons is unique and breathtaking and almost impossible to confine to military targets. Chemical and biological weapons, horrible as they are, cannot match them as agents of catastrophe.

Two months later the highly respected authority on nuclear weaponry, William J. Broad, wrote in the August 3, 2003, issue of *The New*

York Times, "Welcome to the second nuclear age and the Bush administration's quiet response to the age's perceived dangers." He referred to critics who "hate the Bushites' proposal to use mini-nukes, question whether radioactive fallout can be contained and denounce the project's overall secrecy." After all, it had been agreed for decades that nukes would remain under civilian control.

The drastic, threatening change in military doctrine now occurring must be laid directly at President Bush's door. Immediately after his nomination, George W. Bush invited his father's secretary of defense, Dick Cheney, to advise him. After all, George W. Bush had very little experience to qualify him for the presidency, certainly none in the military field. One of Cheney's first assignments was to help determine who should be Bush's running mate for the vice presidency. Lo and behold, it turned out to be Dick Cheney, who rapidly became George W. Bush's alter ego. The public doesn't hear much of Cheney's role, for he knows well the old adage, "Power doesn't come from what you say publicly but by what you whisper in the ear of the leader."

Cheney managed to bring onto the new team many of his colleagues from previous right-wing Republican administrations. First Donald Rumsfeld was selected to be secretary of defense. He was Cheney's longtime friend, former boss and, like Cheney, an earlier secretary of defense. Then came Colin Powell as secretary of state, a four-star general and former chairman of the Joint Chiefs who served under Cheney during the first war against Iraq. Condoleeza Rice, the brilliant, hawkish former colleague of Cheney, was appointed national security adviser. To make sure this team would present a strong militaristic front, proven war hawks were assigned as their deputies: I. Lewis Libby for Cheney, Paul Wolfowitz for Rumsfeld, and Stephen Hadley for Rice. Together this team is a powerful force in the office of the president— a team well experienced and steeped in the power and glory of America's potent military machine. They demonstrated this by launching the major and abrupt changes in our nation's defense policies that I described earlier— thereby greatly irritating many ranking career military officers.

This is not the way America was designed to be. The military was supposed to run our defense programs subject to the counsel and approval of a civilian secretary of defense. The secretary of state and national security adviser were supposed to bring their counsel through the president, and the vice president was only to play a notoriously insignificant role—he was just a standby in case of the president's demise.

The current intelligence fiasco America has suffered has come about primarily because of the Defense Department's deep involvement in trying to find intelligence to support its militaristic policies. Defense, State and National Security should keep out of the intelligence business, leaving that to our independent intelligence agency. Its honesty can be compromised by the intercession of policy considerations.

Nicholas D. Kristof's June 6, 2003, column in *The New York Times* stated, ". . . the Pentagon has become the 800 pound gorilla of the Bush administration, playing a central role in foreign policy and intelligence as well as military matters. . . . My own limited encounters with spies reinforce the idea that intelligence needs to be digested by professionals rather than cherry-picked by ideologues."

More recently, in an article published by *Democracy Now* on August 8, 2003, retired Air Force Lt. Col. Karen Kwiatkowski was quoted as saying, "If one is seeking the answers to why peculiar bits of intelligence found sanctity in a presidential speech, or why the post-Saddam occupation has been distinguished by confusion and false steps, one need not look further than the process inside the office of the secretary of defense." She had worked for over two years, until April 2003, for Under Secretary of Defense for Policy Douglas Feith. She stated that she told her boss that "some folks on the Pentagon's E-ring may find themselves sitting in war-crimes tribunals."

As early as February 2, 2003, James Risin and David Johnstone reported in *The New York Times,* after extensive interviews with government officials, that the Bush administration was distorting intelligence information, and that Deputy Defense Secretary Paul D. Wolfowitz and Deputy National Security Adviser Stephen J. Hadley, who maintained a very good working relationship, indeed were most eager to do so. They cited one official who described the feelings of some analysts in the intelligence agencies as, ". . . more than just skepticism. I think there is also a sense of disappointment with the [intelligence] community's leadership that they are not standing up for them at a time when the evidence is obviously being politicized."

According to Robert Dreyfuss, writing in the July 7, 2003, issue of *The Nation*, an even bigger scandal than politicization of intelligence "is waiting in the wings: the fact that members of the administration failed to produce an intelligence evaluation of what Iraq might look like after the fall of Saddam Hussein. Instead they ignored fears expressed by analysts at the Central Intelligence Agency, the Defense Intelligence Agency and the State Department who predicted that postwar Iraq would be chaotic, violent and ungovernable, and that Iraqis would greet the occupying armies with firearms, not flowers." Melvin Goodman, a former CIA analyst with the Center for International Policy was quoted by Dreyfuss as saying, "I know for a fact that at CIA and NESA [the State Department's Bureau of Near Eastern and South Asian Affairs], none of them thought that postwar Iraq would be governable."

So far events have supported such predictions. Hatred of the American occupiers has led to guerilla warfare, an increase in the number of suicide bombings and more death on both sides. The demand for dollars is mounting and the folly of the White House's prewar dogma is beginning to shine. There are cries for America to withdraw and for someone to be made accountable.

The opposition party in the Congress must do its duty and force an open, televised, Congressional investigation. A secretive review chaired by a Republican Committee Chairman will hardly do.

4

War on the Environment

The current breakdown in integrity at high levels is particularly apparent in the deceitful way the Bush administration, in concert with many business leaders, is staging a war on environmental protection. They do this in spite of wide recognition of the serious threat environmental degradation poses to all life and with cynical disregard for the major efforts being made worldwide to prevent it. The United States was traditionally the leader in this effort. But no longer.

When George W. Bush took office, he became commander in chief of the anti-environment force, ably assisted by the well-proven, stellar anti-environmentalists with whom he surrounded himself: Vice President Dick Cheney, Secretary of Energy Spencer Abraham and Attorney General John Ashcroft, along with their seconds-in-command, and Secretary of the Interior Gale Norton, along with her immediate subordinates. Recently the president appointed Michael O. Leavitt as administrator of EPA. He replaces Christie Todd Whitman, who was not one of them.

Leavitt's anti-environment record as governor of Utah is well known. His attempt to build a 125-mile-long highway across a key Utah wetland has angered conservationists and the 10th Circuit Court of Appeals, which issued a strongly worded decision that, for the time being, stopped construction. Also, according to syndicated columnist Ellen Goodman in her October 10, 2003, column, "On his [Leavitt's] watch, an agreement with the Bush administration took millions of acres of wilderness off the protected list and opened them to development. On his watch the state's clean-water enforcement was tied for dead last. On his watch, environmentalists say they were simply cut out of the decision." Now he is part of an anti-environment team that has nullified many pro-environment programs.

What is this group's motive? Are members ignorant of the growing, scientifically established environmental threats to all life that are now occurring? Or are they simply paying off their self-serving friends and political supporters in business and the religious right who are opposed to environmental regulations? Whatever their objective, their irresponsible actions seriously threaten the quality of life of today's children and future generations. If I were they, I would be deeply worried about how my children and my grandchildren would grade my passage through life.

The League of Conservation Voters graded President Bush on environmental issues after his first three years in office, giving him a big red F. This is the first time they ever gave a president such a dreadful report card. In response, Karl Rove has already put his notorious spin machine to work churning out tales describing President Bush as a good environmentalist.

The current administration's alliance with business, its main source of political funding, is of special concern. Business has been the primary cause of the serious environmental degradation in the past. But without business's strong involvement in solving the problem, the world will never get out of the serious environmental predicament that plagues it. Fortunately, as a result of the passage of environmental laws and regulations, business has been forced to make some changes. Over the past thirty years, through government and business collaboration, great progress has been made in reducing air and water pollution, protecting the earth's ozone shield, stopping production of dangerous pesticides and cleaning up abandoned, polluted manufacturing sites. In the process, a substantial number of businesses discovered that a healthy environment and a healthy economy are mutually supportive and are showing the way in cleaning up and protecting the environment. The DuPont Company is a prime example. The business community should be looking to these enlightened enterprises for leadership, not to the White House.

Yet the world environment is losing ground at an accelerating rate. Air, water, climate, streams, lakes, oceans, croplands, forests, parklands, wetlands, fish and wildlife and humanity are all taking a beating. Norman Meyers, world-renowned ecologist and Oxford University professor, recently wrote, "We face an enormous environmental crisis that is growing bigger at a rapid rate." And the United States, with only 5 percent of the world's people, is in many ways the world's principal environmental culprit. Accordingly the United States needs to play a special role in fighting *for* the environment. This is a global problem that calls for participation by the whole world community. The United States *must resume* its earlier constructive leadership in the United Nations' extensive environmental program. Imagine how irritated our former UN collaborators must have been when 178 nations voted to adopt the Kyoto Protocol to fight global warming and only the United States voted *no*.

The Bush team also brings its penchant and skill for deceit to the environmental arena. One example is its persistent effort to discredit environmentalists in the same way it discredited political opponents. It sees environmentalists as "kooks," "tree huggers," "anti-American," "unscientific," "out of touch" or "hurting the economy." Contrast that to reality. Over eighty million Americans call themselves environmentalists. Ten million of them have joined nongovernment organizations (NGOs), building ever more effective citizen advocacy, legal defense and environmental education programs. A November 8, 2002, poll shows that such NGOs are among the most trusted organizations in the world. They now need to coalesce into one potent force.

Over the past thirty years the American people, using our democratic process, have elected pro-environmental legislators to most local, state and federal legislative bodies, resulting in a stream of environmental laws and regulations, and agencies have been established to enforce them. These laws and regulations were inspired by real-life experience with environmental problems and are based on solid scientific knowledge stemming from university, government and independent laboratories, and from the national academies of science, engineering and medicine. Science is the backbone and foundation of the environmental movement.

Many business leaders now agree that pollution prevention pays. Many religions are teaching that the Earth is threatened by human activities and calling for their members to work to "be stewards of God's creation." The United Nations has become a vital player, and increasing numbers of students are earning degrees in environmental studies, environmental science, environmental law and ecology. These young people have gone on to influential positions in business, government and public interest organizations, thereby educating others.

A culture of environmentalism now permeates America and much of the world. It is an inclusive culture that has the potential to bring the peoples of the world closer together. And it is a force that will roll over those hard-right anti-environmentalists who are making a last ditch stand based on misinformation and deception. The sooner we the people can bring this force to bear, the more tomorrow's children will respect us.

The White House is not the only problem. Congress too is at fault. The number of anti-environment, right-wing Republicans there has grown until, in the 1999-2000 session, there were eighty-four of them, including all Republican leaders, who scored zero on environmental issues as measured by the League of Conservation Voters. Not one Democrat earned such a dismal score. Fortunately President Clinton blocked most of their anti-environment actions. But when George W. Bush became president, he gave the right wing what it wanted. The auto, oil, coal and utility businesses cheered him on. After all, these companies in particular have been vigorously fighting environmental regulations for years, building ever more potent and expensive advertising and lobbying programs to influence the American people and their government. This behavior goes back to the early 1970s when the auto industry attacked the Clean Air Act, contending the act's control of auto emissions would ruin the industry and cost hundreds of thousands of jobs. But when passed, this act led to the development of the catalytic converter, which added hundreds of thousands of jobs, primarily in the auto industry.

In the mid-1970s, when inflation rose to 13 percent, a number of captains of industry personally launched a campaign, without any supporting data, claiming that environmental regulations were a principal cause. Within two years, government and private studies clearly proved that the maximum impact of the regulations had to be less than one-half of 1 percent, as environmentalists had contended. Over the years this destructive, self-serving smoke screen used by some powerful businesses has intensified. And since the White House and its colleagues in Congress have now joined this effort, the situation is serious indeed. A current example is the all-out effort to belittle the threat of global warming and to block actions to reduce the threat in spite of overwhelming worldwide scientific evidence, the support of all other members of the United Nations and increasing observations of current serious impacts of climate change. That's not what we ought to expect from a country that, with only 5 percent of the world's people, emits 25 percent of global emissions of the greenhouse gas carbon dioxide.

Other recent examples are:

•The reckless, unsubstantiated exaggeration of potential job loss used by the auto companies to successfully block Congress from enacting higher auto fuel efficiency standards.

•The even more extreme distortion by auto and oil companies that claim, with no supporting evidence, that "hundreds of thousands of jobs" would be created by drilling for oil in the Arctic National Wildlife Refuge.

•The unsuccessful attempt by the Alliance of Automobile Manufacturers to block California's passage of a bill that limits greenhouse gas emissions from cars and light trucks. The auto companies once again claimed the legislation would cost "hundreds of thousands of jobs." They are notorious for such wild predictions of job loss to mobilize their workers into joining their major lobbying campaigns. And when their claims subsequently are shown to be false, they don't apologize. They just do it again.

The Bush administration's record of marching in lockstep with business to devastate the environment is the worst in history. Among other things, it has opened our treasures of national parks, refuges, forests and wilderness areas to exploitation; adopted an environmentally damaging energy plan defined by the oil, coal, gas and nuclear industries; relaxed provisions of the Clean Air Act and Clean Water Act at the behest of industry; used the temporary fallout from the manipulation of the California energy market by Enron and others to declare a (non-existent) national energy crisis, thereby justifying more oil drilling; effectively turned over to business the administration's powerful Office of Information and Regulatory Affairs; and begun to dismantle the National Environment Policy Act, America's Magna Carta for the environment.

The Bush administration's contempt for the environment can also be seen in the names it gives its programs:

•It designs a program to weaken the Clean Air Act and calls it the "Clear Skies" initiative.

•It opens the door for the logging industry to clear cut its way through our forests and names it the "Healthy Forests" initiative.

•It promotes an "Energy Security" plan which would give billions of dollars in tax breaks to the oil and gas industries.

•It concocts the "Freedom Car" which has nothing to do with freedom but everything to do with postponing for a decade America's facing up to the auto industry's outrageous but highly profitable love affair with gas guzzlers.

And so it goes—its attitude is clearly "to hell with the environment."

Not only does our Department of Defense run rampant with its continued buildup of history's most powerful war machine, but now Secretary Rumsfeld, complaining that pro-environment laws compromise readiness, is seeking permanent blanket exemption from *all* of them.

As an example of the serious threat posed by these extremists, let me quote from one of them, David Horowitz, writing in *Front Page* magazine: "Why should this siege against science and good sense [environmental regulations] be lifted only when and where it impacts the military? The armed forces could burnish their credentials as freedom's defenders if they fought this battle on a broader front."

In contrast, here are the words of J. William Futrell (*The Environmental Forum*, May/June 2003) about the full-scale attack on environmental regulations now underway. He wrote this upon his retirement after twenty-three years as the dedicated, non-partisan president of the Environmental Law Institute, which has played a key role in the creation, advancement and protection of environmental law nationally and internationally. Futrell believes that America is "abandoning its leadership in environmental diplomacy," and that:

America's legacy of robust environmental law is in jeopardy. Premodern dogma of radical federalism and unfettered commerce are being revived to attack not just environmental laws, but the constitutional foundation on which they stand. Some advocates and judges hold that our Constitution demands massive deregulation, special rights for corporations and developers, and curtailment of citizen access to justice. Yet the nation's great body of environmental law forms the idea base, the ethical and moral standards that will govern humanity's use of the environment for the long term. Together we've expanded consciousness of environmental law and of its greatest achievement: the codification of a change of ethics, a recognition that government and individual responsibility extend to the natural world.

Another dedicated environmentalist, Vawter Parker, executive director of Earth Justice, put it this way in his June 2003 letter, "President Bush has made lax enforcement of our environmental laws a hallmark of his administration. Powerful special interests—led by big oil, gas, mining and timber companies—are using their ever-tightening grip on Washington to weaken environmental laws and sharply curtail the enforcement of those laws. If they succeed, decades of environmental progress will be lost and our ability to protect America's natural heritage will be weakened for years to come."

The development and use of energy are the biggest threats to our nation's environment. The oil, coal, nuclear and auto industries involved are huge, powerful and profitable, and are run by executives who fiercely oppose environmental regulations. They are working in concert with the former energy company executives who now run our federal government.

The technologies required for using more environmentally friendly sources of energy *have been developed* and their effectiveness demonstrated on fairly large scales. The best bet is the so-called soft-energy path. It involves using energy more efficiently and developing renewable forms of energy such as wind and solar. Opportunities for doing so are abundant. It is a win-win situation, but *we need the right leadership to provide the necessary incentives to jump-start these developments.* Good progress was made during President Carter's term, but then President Reagan pulled the plug. Other countries, providing incentives, are now moving rapidly with these new technologies, particularly in Europe and especially with wind energy. Some private companies in the United States also are starting to move with wind energy. But the Bush administration has cut the budget for developing renewable energy while markedly increasing it for oil, coal and nuclear.

With the whole structure of our nation's environmental protection at risk, why isn't the environment at the top of every American's concerns? After all, eighty million of us call ourselves environmentalists and ten million are members of activist organizations. The only thing more important than the quality of our lives is the quality of our children's lives. We and the generations who will follow are fundamentally dependent upon the basic supports of life—air, water, food, sunlight, climate, plants, animals and the wondrous and inspiring landscapes around us. All are nurtured by environmental protection.

One answer might be that most environmental issues aren't immediate in the same way that a tax reduction is. They involve the future. Another answer is that the people with the biggest bully pulpits, like the president and his team, are either belittling environmentalism or not mentioning it. The big problem is that almost no one with a significant bully pulpit is telling the American people the truth about the seriousness and urgency of current threats to the environment stemming from the decisions made by right-wing Republicans now running our national government. We need to find such a spokesman, an environmental Paul Revere. When we do, American patriots will rise up and retake their government.

Do you doubt that the current state of our environment is a matter of concern? If so, I suggest that you:

•Visit your hospital's emergency room during an air-quality alert and make note of the number of children and adults who are there due to allergies or asthma caused or aggravated by air pollution.

•Have your home drinking water checked for contaminants.

•Try to find a stream that really is swimmable.

•Take your family to Yellowstone National Park this winter to see firsthand how swarms of snowmobiles are damaging it.

•Fly over American cities and observe the haze that all that too often obscures them.

•Visit our spectacular Glacier National Park before 2030, when its glaciers will be gone due to global warming.

•See the inspiring, towering, thousand-year-old Sequoias before a timber company fells them.

•Count the declining number and variety of birds that migrate in spring and fall.

•Visit fishermen anywhere and learn of the devastation now occurring in our fisheries.

•Join a nature group to see the wonders around you and learn what is threatening them.

And then in contrast, read how some large companies *are* demonstrating that industry can prosper while markedly reducing pollutants, waste and use of virgin space. Take a ride in a "green" car like the Toyota Prius, which gets forty-five to fifty miles per gallon. Visit a wind farm on the Pacific coast and learn how many companies are converting free wind to electricity.

Above all, don't leave the whole job of saving the environment to our children and future generations. Now is the time to take inventory of the natural treasures still around you—and then do battle to protect them.

5

Going-It-Alone:
The United States versus the World

Americans, with the exception of American Indians, descend from immigrants from foreign lands. We are a sampling of all of the peoples of the world. In this diversity lies our strength. In this we demonstrate how people from everywhere can live together in freedom and prosperity with justice under law. This is the American way of life.

Some of our forebears dreamed of a world community where people could live together in harmony and constructive partnership. President Woodrow Wilson was one. He led the post-World War I effort that created the League of Nations. The League failed to reach the idealistic goals Wilson had set for it primarily because his own country didn't support him. The League did, however, provide an association that worked together on common issues and served as a sounding board for its members. After the slaughter and destruction of World War II, the desire for an assembly of nations that could advance the cause of world peace and a decent quality of life mounted. This time America played the key role in bringing about and supporting the United Nations.

Current UN Secretary General and Nobel Laureate Kofi Annan has said of the United Nations: "Despite the sense of vulnerability and uncertainty that pervades the global consciousness, people and nations retain the hope of uniting around a common humanity. . . . They look for ways to translate into reality the ideals expressed in the United Nations Charter, which established the fundamental principles of international law."

That charter, which describes the principles to which the United States committed itself, was established at an international meeting in 1945 in San Francisco and reads in part:

> We the peoples of the United Nations determined to save succeeding generations from the scourge of war which twice in our lifetime has brought untold sorrow to mankind and to reaffirm faith in fundamental human rights, in the dignity and worth of the human person, in the equal rights of men and women and of nations large and small, and to establish conditions under which justice and respect for the obligations arising from treaties and other sources of international law can be maintained, and to promote social progress and better standards of life in larger freedom, *and for these ends* to practice tolerance and life together in peace with one another as good neighbors and to unite our strength to maintain international peace and security, and to ensure by the acceptance of principles and the institution of methods, that armed force shall not be used, save in the common interest, and to employ international machinery for the promotion of the economic and social advancement of all peoples, *have resolved to combine our efforts to accomplish these aims.* Accordingly our respective governments do hereby establish an international organization to be known as the United Nations. [italics mine]

Now after fifty-eight years, essentially all the nations of the world (nearly two hundred) are members. I believe any objective evaluation must declare the United Nations a great success. Every citizen of the world belongs. One person, the secretary general of the United Nations, can speak for us all. Each nation participates and votes on issues. Through membership each nation becomes well informed of the key problems now facing humanity and the environment, as well as routes to solving them. Collectively, human and financial resources are brought to bear. The eradication of disease, the advancement of peace-keeping and the protection of the earth's environment are priorities. And throughout the life of the United Nations, the United States has been an inspiring leader, a key provider of funds and personnel, and has earned the friendship of people everywhere.

I have had the opportunity to participate in a number of United Nations activities and as a leader in several international public interest organizations. What a rewarding experience that has been—getting to know and communicate with people from all over the world. Today uncounted thousands of Americans have had somewhat similar experiences through regularly networking by e-mail with friends from other lands. Such communications have been warm and positive until recently. Now they ask disturbingly, "What has happened to America's integrity? Can't you do something about it?"

I answer, "Yes we can. And we will."

The problem stems from the Bush administration's turning its back on the United Nations. As a result, the most powerful and most fortunately endowed nation has now earned the world's hostility, adding impetus to growing violence against America. President Bush boldly told the rest of the world, "If you are not with us, you are against us," but he failed to recognize that the world is sending the same message to us. Secretary General Annan has said that the United States is "practically standing alone in opposition to agreements that were broadly reached by about everyone else," and calls on us to "close ranks with the rest of the international community."

Thirteen examples of such dereliction by the Bush administration in its first two years follow:

•The International Criminal Court was created in 1998 to establish an international body to prosecute genocide, war crimes and crimes against humanity. This court is now in effect, having been ratified by sixty-eight nations. But the United States is not one of them. President Clinton signed the treaty but President Bush canceled Clinton's approval, thereby blocking its potential ratification by the Senate. The president wants blanket immunity for all U.S. citizens. When thirty-five countries that had signed the treaty refused to give the United States immunity, the president suspended U.S. aid to those countries.
•In July 2001, a United Nations Conference on global warming voted 178 to 1 to proceed with the Kyoto Protocol. Guess who voted no, even though we had played a key role in the creation of the Protocol?
•Nearly all nations are convinced that population growth is one of the world's most serious problems and recognize that family planning— a means to help women avoid unwanted pregnancies—is a key solution. Over many years the United States, with bipartisan support, has provided leadership and funding for this highly successful effort.

But now President Bush at the behest of the religious right has stopped the payment of funds already appropriated for family planning in developing countries. UN officials estimate that the loss of such funds could lead not only to accelerated population growth, but also to 800,000 more abortions, as well as the deaths of numerous mothers and children.

•The Convention on the Rights of the Child has been ratified by 191 countries. Only the United States and Somalia are holdouts.

•The United Nation's Convention on the Elimination of All Forms of Discrimination Against Women has been ratified by 170 nations—but not the United States

•Limbs and lives are lost almost daily by civilians in countries around the world due to contact with one of the many millions of land mines strewn over the countryside during military conflicts. Well over one hundred countries have signed the Convention on the Prohibition of the Use, Stockpiling, Production and Transfer of Anti-Personnel Mines and on their Destruction. But the United States, the supreme military power, refuses to sign, arguing that land mines are necessary for its military operations.

•The United States in July 2002 attempted but failed to block a UN anti-torture plan strongly supported by European and Latin American allies.

•The Bush administration is withdrawing systematically from UN peacekeeping operations for which the United States has been the key supporter.

•At the same time our super-powerful, greedy, military weapons industry, with the blessing of our government, floods the world, especially developing countries, with military sales totaling more than the combined arms sales of all other countries. Much—such as the $6.4 billion sale in the year 2000 of eighty F-16 fighter jets to the United Arab Emirates—goes to the Arab world.

•President Bush and his warrior team, with overwhelming military force, invaded nearly defenseless Iraq after using a string of fallacious reasons for doing so, and after failing to gain the support of the United Nations. Although the world appreciated getting rid of the brutal Saddam Hussein regime, the Bush administration's method of doing it was broadly condemned.

•With encouragement from tobacco companies, the United States fought against a tobacco-control treaty that was subsequently approved by the World Health Assembly. On the eve of the final negotiating session, the United States tried unsuccessfully to undermine the agreement by exempting countries from any actions with which they disagreed. Whether the United States, whose citizens demand control of tobacco at home, will sign and ratify the treaty that does so globally, is questionable.

•The Bush administration is irritating the World Trade Organization and threatening international trade by reneging on world-trade agreements.

•The Alien Tort Claims Act, adopted over two hundred years ago, has been an effective international agreement for suing violators of human rights abroad. Now under pressure from oil and gas companies that want to be exempt from human rights abuses in foreign lands, the U.S. Justice Department is trying to get around the Alien Tort Claims Act.

This serious retreat from major international agreements and treaties has been especially irritating to other developed countries that once worked in conjunction with the United States to establish them in the first place. This is especially true for members of the European Union, formerly our most trusted and cooperative allies.

Ronald Brownstein of *The Los Angeles Times* discussed this issue in his May 8, 2003, column: "Europe strikes a very different balance than the United States between individual freedom and the common good. In their domestic politics, Europeans have been more willing than Americans to accept limits on their individual choices to build a stronger common community. In direct extension they are more willing than President Bush to accept limits on national sovereignty to create a more cohesive international community."

Brownstein goes on to say that this difference in philosophy explains why Europe more strongly supports the United Nations; why in contrast to Europe, Bush fights the Kyoto Treaty, cuts taxes deeply, thereby "eviscerating government revenues that support activities society can only undertake collectively"; promotes individual choice in Social Security and Medicare programs which "would almost certainly diminish the universal benefit guaranteed to all"; plans a similar approval in health care "at the price of eroding the collective guarantee of decent care for all of the insured." Conversely, "In Europe the dominant opinion sees a value in strengthening collective institutions—domestically and internationally—even when that constrains individual choices." Brownstein asserts that even if Bush and European leaders talk of reconciling, "the chasm between them—less on the use of force than on the value of collective action—virtually guarantees more storms across the Atlantic."

The chasm Brownstein refers to was greatly deepened when Europe realized that America's reasons for going to war with Iraq were phony. This naturally led to the suspicion that our hidden agenda was gaining control of Mideast oil. This suspicion continues to grow, showing how deceiving one's friends can backfire. Europe won't be fooled again.

Yet we need Europe and Europe needs us, and the world needs us both. The problem of global warming provides a good example. It is quintessentially a global problem. The world scientific community almost unanimously agrees that the problem is real, that it is caused at least in part by human activities and that it is growing. Glaciers and low-lying coastal areas are receding as temperatures and sea levels rise. Storms are more severe, drought more frequent and flooding more devastating. All may be the result of global warming. And the United States and Europe, with their high standards of living, are most culpable because of their disproportionate generation of greenhouse gases.

When informed of these environmental changes, our president was childish to say, "I don't believe it," and later "I now believe it, but we will have to learn to live with it." We must convince him to think differently or replace him. The world's future demands our doing so.

Maybe the president's buddy Tony Blair can convince President Bush of the reality of environmental problems. Prime Minister Blair is deeply concerned about the threat of global warming, speaks out regularly and forcefully on the issue and has placed his country firmly behind the Kyoto Protocol that sets dates and goals for countries to reduce greenhouse gas emissions.

Other national and world leaders also have an acute awareness of the need for setting a good example, for cooperating with and understanding other nations as the interdependence of our global neighborhood becomes increasingly apparent. Here is what several of them said to young people graduating from college this past spring:

Nobel Peace Prize Winner, Archbishop Desmond M. Tutu, in his commencement address at the University of Pennsylvania, stated, "You in this country helped us to become free, you helped us to become democratic, you helped us to become a country that is seeking to be non-racial and non-sexist. You didn't bomb us into liberation. We became free nonviolently. And the country demonstrated that there are other ways of dealing with difference, with disagreement, with conflict. The way of forgiveness, the way of compromise, the way of reconciliation. And we learned in South Africa that there is no way in which you are going to have true security that comes from the barrel of a gun."

George J. Tenet, director of the Central Intelligence Agency, speaking at the University of Oklahoma's commencement, reminded graduates that, "Today, the United States is the lone superpower, with global interests and worldwide reach—part of everyone's problem and everyone's solution. And by this I mean more than Afghanistan and Iraq, where crises called forth from us a military response. There is another, underlying story that must be told: the story of societies and peoples who are left behind, excluded from the benefits of an expanding global economy, whose lives of hunger, disease, and displacement may become wellsprings of disaffection and extremism."

Secretary General Kofi Annan reminded this year's Duke graduates that, "As someone once said about water pollution, we all live downstream. This interdependence generates a host of new and urgent demands. Towns and villages have their planning boards, fire departments and recycling centers. Nations have their legislatures and judicial bodies. Our globalizing world also needs institutions and standards. I am not talking about world government; such an idea never was, and never could be, either practical or desirable. I mean laws and norms that countries negotiate together, and agree to uphold as the 'rules of the road.' And I mean a forum where sovereign states can come together to share burdens, address common problems and seize common opportunities."

Queen Noor of Jordan, at William and Mary's commencement, also spoke of the need for interdependence. "We live in a time when it is critically important to build such coalitions, but on very different terms—not an axis of self-interest between states for political ends, but true partnerships between people based on respect for our shared values, needs and fundamental human rights, and also on respect for our differences. And these coalitions would apply not only to my region, important as it is right now, but from Afghanistan to the Balkans, the Middle East to East Timor, Northern Ireland to Rwanda even here in the United States—anywhere anyone is struggling to overcome conflict and inequity."

Senator Patrick Leahy of Vermont, addressing Norwich University graduates, reminded them that, "History has shown that nations with unmatched military power have, time and again, made tragic mistakes that have led to their downfall. The Romans, the Ottomans, and the Soviet Union are but a few. Some of these governments became so obsessed with extending their empires far beyond their borders that their core values as a society withered and the outside world, or their own people, turned violently against them."

What a contrast these five speakers provide in tone and theme to this excerpt from Vice President Cheney's speech to the Class of 2003 at West Point. "The battle of Iraq was a major victory in the war on terror, but the war itself is far from over. We cannot allow ourselves to grow complacent. We cannot forget that the terrorists remain determined to kill as many Americans as possible, both abroad and here at home, and they are still seeking weapons of mass destruction to use against us. With such an enemy, no peace treaty is possible; no policy of containment or deterrence will prove effective. The only way to deal with this threat is to destroy it, completely and utterly."

The vice president neglected to admit to his audience that the world now knows that the battle of Iraq had nothing to do with the war on terror, except to augment the recruitment of increasing numbers of terrorists around the globe.

Hans Blix of Sweden, recently retired Chief UN Weapons Inspector, expressed some of his reactions and concerns to Felicity Berringer of *The New York Times*. In an article published June 19, 2003, she quotes Blix as saying: "What surprised me, what amazes me, is that it seems the military people were expecting to stumble on large quantities of gas, chemical weapons and biological weapons. I don't see how they could have come to such an attitude if they had, at any time, studied the reports of present and former United Nations inspectors. Is the United Nations on a different planet? Are reports from here totally unread south of the Hudson?"

Asked about the war's outcome, Mr. Blix replied, "We all welcome the disappearance of one of the world's most horrible regimes." But he also noted that the increasing anti-Americanism in the Middle East and the fact that the United States continues to distance itself from the UN Security Council were huge negatives.

When asked about David Kay, who was sent to Iraq by the Bush administration to advise the U.S. inspection teams, and who had worked for Blix as an inspector when he was director general of the International Atomic Energy Agency, Blix related his own falling out with Kay, who "distorted his record of inspecting Iraq's nuclear facilities." Reading this, one has to ask, is Kay the right man for the job?

Professor Jared Diamond of the University of California at Los Angeles would have made a good commencement speaker. In an op-ed piece in *The Los Angeles Times* on June 22, 2003, he describes the history of the Fertile Crescent, the territory now known as Iraq, Syria, Iran and Jordan. Capitalizing on the superb environment of the Tigris and Euphrates rivers, fertile soil, lush forests, Mediterranean climate and an abundance of wild plants and animals, those who lived there built "the world center of wealth, power and civilization." Over the centuries "they inadvertently destroyed the environmental resources on which their society depended. . . . They had the misfortune to be living in an extremely fragile environment, which because of its low rainfall was particularly susceptible to deforestation. The end product of this history is people poor in everything but oil."

Professor Diamond recommends the world community intervene *before* the next crisis: "The most effective and least expensive approach would be to help Third World countries solve their basic environmental and public health problems before they cripple their societies." He suggests that President Bush aim at preempting such crises, rather than at preempting military aggression.

But the United States can't do that alone. This is where the United Nations comes in. Defining crises, developing programs to address them and enlisting the whole world to help in these processes is its central tenet. At his July 30, 2003, news conference, Secretary General Kofi Annan argued against President Bush's claim that the United Nations might become irrelevant. Describing the conference, Felicity Berringer wrote that Annan described the value of international institutions in general and the United Nations in particular when he said, "Many of us sense that we are living through a crisis of the international system . . . forcing us to ask ourselves whether the institutions and methods we are accustomed to are really adequate to deal with all the stresses of the last couple of years."

Annan indicated his own support for a new Security Council resolution on Iraq "creating a broader international framework for restoring security and rebuilding political institutions." He appeared pleased to say, "I did warn those who were bashing the UN that they had to be careful because they may need the UN soon."

The United States clearly needs the UN in Iraq now, as I discussed earlier. It is good that Bush's rare multilateralist, Secretary of State Colin Powell, has finally gone, hat in hand, to the United Nations asking for help. But the extremists in the administration don't like it. Their view was expressed by one of their prime mouthpieces, columnist George Will, who recently claimed that "a core principle of conservatism is to preserve U.S. sovereignty and freedom of action by marginalizing the United Nations."

We patriots need to fight such nonsense and see that our country gets back to assuming its proper role as a key player in the United Nations' collective effort. By working together we can get the job done and regain the respect, admiration and constructive companionship of our fellow citizens of Earth.

6

From Love to Hate

It is a huge tragedy for America that the Bush administration has managed to turn upside down the benign image the United States has traditionally held in the world. Like it or not, in a span of less than three years, America has gone from being perceived as friend and partner to being viewed as the enemy, scrooge and a loner. The transformation is disturbing and foreboding. The record clearly shows, however, that this negative image is well earned, as illustrated in the foregoing chapters.

In mid-2003, the Pew Research Center for the People and the Press released a survey that found "the [Iraq] war has widened the rift between Americans and Western Europeans, further inflamed the Muslim world, softened support for the war on terrorism and significantly weakened global public support for the pillars of the post-World War II era—the UN and the North Atlantic Alliance." The poll showed:

•"Favorable views of the United States have declined in nearly every country" since summer 2002. Our unilateral foreign policy is a prime concern.

•Some of the sharpest turns in public opinion took place in Western Europe. Over 60 percent in France, Germany, Russia and Spain had a favorable view of the United States one year ago. Now it is respectively 13 percent, 45 percent, 36 percent and 38 percent.

•Over 70 percent of the people in Russia, Turkey, Indonesia, Pakistan and Nigeria thought the United States could become a threat to their country.

•The Muslim countries were concerned that Islam itself could be in jeopardy.

In his *New York Times* column on June 1, 2003, Thomas Friedman develops another reason why non-Americans hate us: "During the 1990's, America became exponentially more powerful—economically, militarily and technologically—than any other country in the world, if not in history." Its power "became so dominant that America began to touch people's lives around the planet more than their own governments. In response, they began organizing, saying in essence, "I want to have a vote on how your power is exercised because it's a force shaping my life."

Then came 9/11, turning America into what Friedman calls "a wounded, angry, raging beast touching people militarily. Now people become really frightened of us, an attitude reenforced by the Bush team's unilateralism and its smashing of the Taliban and Iraq in short order. People around the world communicate their outrage and build alliances that oppose America on the Internet, fanning the current global anti-Americanism. With the continuing rapid growth of the Internet and the global networking facilities, more and more potent, non-government worldwide alliances may be spawned, able, they hope, to tie up superpowers—especially America."

Nicholas Kristof, in *The New York Times*, January 31, 2003, yearned "for the halcyon days of a year ago, when we fretted about why Arabs hate us. Now the question is, why does everybody hate us? Does it matter that we've somehow morphed in public perception from the world's only superpower to the world's super-rogue state?"

Responding to his own questions, he writes, "The macho notion that we'll do what we choose and if the world doesn't like it, it can go to hell is both ludicrous and dangerous. We mustn't become slaves to foreign opinion, but neither should we glibly dismiss it."

Nevertheless we did and we continue to dismiss it, as when President Bush elected not to attend the 2002 World Congress on the Environment. Enviromnental leaders and lovers of the natural world have been meeting every ten years since 1972 and have found the conference highly constructive and inspiring. I played a role in convincing the UN Secretary General to make the 1992 conference a summit, calling for heads of state to lead their delegations. Nearly every country did so. The elder President Bush represented America and was cheered when he spoke.

Then came 2002. George W. Bush, apparently sensing the world's irritation at his flouting of international environmental commitments, chose not to attend. Instead he sent Secretary of State Colin Powell. Powell, who had achieved a position of respect at the UN, was booed unmercifully; the audience apparently was trying in this way to send a message to President Bush. Other U.S. participants experienced a substantial coolness in their contacts with longtime friends from other countries.

To add fuel to this fire, the current administration has irritated the world community further by not distancing itself from the disgraceful anti-Islam proclamations issued by leaders of the religious right, including Jerry Falwell, Pat Robertson, Franklin Graham and Jerry Vines. Two examples of their insensitivity come to mind: Vines has never been taken to task for calling the prophet Mohammed a "demon-possessed pedophile." And Graham has preached that Islam is "a very evil and wicked religion." These conservative Christians are avid supporters of the right wingers running our government. Their preaching has stimulated efforts by American evangelical Christians to convince Muslims to embrace Jesus. Apparently they don't know that Muslims have already accepted Jesus as a prophet. Nor do they show concern that their aggressive missionary efforts are angering increasing numbers of the billion-plus Muslims. No wonder the Muslim-dominated countries hate us.

If America hopes to ever regain the respect and cooperation of the rest of the world, it must forego its current love affair with unilateral control; rejoin the family of nations, the United Nations; work cooperatively to solve common problems; and show respect for other nations' roles and religions.

7

The Bush Doctrine: Deliberately Plunging Into Debt and Demeaning the Needy

The Bush administration's economic policy has little to do with growth and jobs, as it contends. The policy has everything to do with its ideology. What is that ideology? Social programs must be curbed, and the way to do that is to cut taxes and starve the government of funds.

This ideology has been around in right-wing Republican circles for a long time. I encountered it forty years ago when I first became involved in politics. It was an insignificant factor then, but over the years it has grown steadily, becoming an appreciable force in the Reagan administration. It led to that administration's binge of cutting taxes and pouring billions into the military, thereby manufacturing deficits. During the following administration, that of George H. W. Bush, the U.S. deficit rose to its highest level in history up to that time.

When Bill Clinton defeated the first President Bush, the right-wing Republican extremists went into a rage. They markedly expanded their think tanks and publications, built what Hilary Clinton called a "vast right-wing conspiracy" and went all out to destroy the Clinton administration, using whatever dirty tricks served their purpose. To learn more about this group, read David Brock's *Blinded by the Right*. Brock was one of their heros but his conscience, as I mentioned earlier, led him to expose in great detail the members of this gang and their machinations.

The Republican extremists were a major force in the election of George W. Bush, and now their ideology and their cohorts dominate his administration. Consider what they have done deliberately to plunge our country into the red: After having inherited a projected ten-year surplus of 5.6 trillion dollars from the Clinton administration, they created a 2003 deficit of almost $400 billion, the highest in history. Now President George W. Bush and his father hold the number one and the number two positions as America's greatest budget busters.

How did George W. Bush earn his title in less than three years after starting with a large surplus? In each of those years, he fathered huge tax cuts that will total more than $4 trillion over the next ten years, as claimed by Goldman Sachs and others. According to the Center of Defense Information, George W. Bush has also increased the military budget from its 2001 level of $310 billion to $400 billion in 2004, not counting the huge, upcoming expenses for reconstructing Iraq. Russia, the second largest spender, has a 2004 budget of $65 billion. The U.S. budget is twenty times the combined budgets of our seven most likely adversaries.

On top of that the president vouches he will sign a prescription drug bill that will cost over $400 billion in the next ten years with no provision for funding it—another huge commitment to financing with borrowed dollars. What a contrast to the lifestyle most of us have learned and honored: to live within our means. To pay our obligations on time. To remember that a penny saved is a penny earned—a penny that might be put toward our children's education or toward our own retirement. If a business operates beyond its means, it goes bankrupt. If an individual doesn't make his credit card payments, he forfeits cards and credit rating. A person who fails to pay his monthly mortgage may lose his house. We the people have a history of requiring that each year's state budget in all fifty states be balanced. Why, then, does the Bush administration flout this wisdom by deliberately operating in the red, plunging our country into deeper debt and ignoring our obligations to future generations?

The answer is that the president and his gang know what they are doing. To keep the voters with him, he goes on a nationwide crusade to convince them to believe that the Bush tax-cutting program will be great for jobs and growth. Speaking before large, televised meetings with big signs behind him proclaiming GROWTH AND JOBS, the president repeatedly preaches this promise to his fellow Americans. This is a Karl Rove tactic: use the bully pulpit to proclaim the message on big banners; repeat it over and over so that the people will believe it, even though there is no truth to it. What the president doesn't tell his listeners is that his tax cuts go predominantly to the wealthy and that one dollar of tax relief for the wealthy will have only a small fraction of the job-creating impact that same dollar would have if it went to the needy. Nor does he tell them that most independent analysts consider his estimate of job gains to be way off the mark. The president either doesn't recognize or doesn't care about the catastrophic consequences of his economic program.

The Concord Coalition, a group of distinguished Americans co-chaired by two senators, one a Democrat and one a Republican, was created in 1992 "to tell America the truth about the tough choices we have to make: to rein in runaway deficits, to make Social Security and Medicare sustainable and to reduce the crushing debt burden we were compiling for future generations." The coalition was generally credited with changing the tone of fiscal responsibility in Washington during the 1990s and in influencing the president and Congress to move from deep deficits and mounting debt to large surpluses, debt reduction and serious discussion of the long term financing of Social Security and Medicare.

Now after two-and-one-half years of the Bush administration, the Coalition gives it a grade of F because of irresponsible fiscal management, for completely reversing the positive trends of the late 1990s. It found the Bush team *guilty of deficits, deception and denial. Deception* because the legislation calls for all of their tax cuts to terminate over the next ten years. You know and they know this will never happen. Can you imagine a future Congress and president abruptly approving such a huge tax increase? *Denial* because they closed their eyes to the inevitable cost of reforming the alternative minimum tax, the growing costs of the Iraq war and the war against terrorism, and the costs of dealing with the unfunded benefit promises of Social Security and Medicare.

For good advice, consider what three of our most successful practitioners of the free enterprise system and sound fiscal management have had to say about right-wing federal management. In an op-ed piece that appeared in the May 23, 2003, Wilmington *News Journal*, Warren Buffett stated, "The rich do indeed get richer. Nonetheless, the Senate voted last week to supply major aid to the rich in their pursuit of ever greater wealth. . . . Instead, give reductions to those who both need and will spend the money gained. Putting $1,000 in the pockets of 310,000 families with urgent needs is going to provide far more stimulus to the economy than putting the same $310 million

[the amount he would gain by eliminating tax on dividends] in my pockets."
He added, "Supporters of making dividends tax free like to paint critics as
promoters of class warfare. The fact is, however, that their proposal promotes
class welfare. For my class."

In regard to the sunset provision in the federal tax bills Buffett stated,
"It's hard to conceive of anything sillier. . . . The first President Bush had a
name for such activities: 'voodoo economics.' It is Enron-style accounting."

George Soros, another American billionaire, said, "The tax cut is
basically redistributing income to the wealthy."

Peter G. Peterson, former secretary of commerce under President
Nixon, frequent presidential advisor and noted financier, wrote in the June 8,
2003, issue of *The New York Times Magazine*:

> I have belonged to the Republican Party all my life. Among the
> bedrock principles that the Republican Party has stood for since its
> origins in the 1850s is the principle of fiscal stewardship—the idea
> that government should invest in posterity and safeguard future
> generations from unsustainable liabilities. . . . Over the past quarter
> century . . . the G.O.P. leadership has by degrees come to embrace a
> very different notion that deficit spending is a sort of fiscal wonder
> drug. . . . Since 2001, the fiscal strategizing of the party has ascended
> to a new level of fiscal irresponsibility. For the first time ever, a
> Republican leadership in complete control of our national
> government is advocating a huge and virtually endless policy of debt
> creation. The numbers are simply breathtaking.

The right-wing Republican extremists' financial theories are not new.
They were first welcomed in the Reagan White House, but not then in the
Congress. President Reagan's budget director, David A. Stockman, wrote in
his 1986 book, *The Triumph of Politics*:

> The 1983 deficit had now already come in at $208 billion. The case
> for a major tax increase was overwhelming, unassailable, inescapable
> and self-evident. Not to raise taxes when all other avenues were closed
> was a wilful act of ignorance and grotesque irresponsibility. In the
> entire 20th century fiscal history of the nation there has been nothing

to rival it. . . . The next day I told Jim Baker [Reagan's chief of staff] that I was going to resign. I couldn't defend any taxes; I couldn't defend a planned trillion dollar deficit; I couldn't defend a policy of fiscal knownothingism. "I can't make a fool of myself any longer, Jim." I told him, "This budget is so bad, it's beyond the pale."

The London Times, so highly respected in British business circles, has said of the current Bush tax-cutting program: "The lunatics are now in charge of the asylum. . . . The more extreme Republicans actually want a fiscal train wreck. Proposing to slash federal spending, particularly on social programs, is a tricky electoral proposition, but a fiscal crisis offers the tantalizing prospect of forcing such cuts through the back door."

The Bush administration has already moved so far toward implementing its radical agenda that at least one of the early conspirators who launched this extreme movement now feels free to brag publicly about what has been accomplished. He is Grover Norquist, a firebrand in the movement for twenty-five years, a partner with Newt Gingrich in his attempt to hijack the federal government, a stalwart in the American Enterprise Institute, president of Americans for Tax Reform, which designed the Bush tax program, and chairman of a weekly gathering of the right-wing elite. This past June, the *Washington Post* ran an op-ed article by Norquist which laid out, step by step, the far right's tax agenda.

Writing on June 17, 2003, in the same newspaper, David Broder quoted Norquist as saying, "We don't have to try to operate under the radar screen [anymore]. We can be very open about our agenda." When Broder asked him what the White House had thought of his op-ed piece, Norquist responded, "They didn't ask me to do it, but they certainly didn't complain about what I did. I have exchanged several e-mails with Karl Rove since then and it's never come up." He added, "I think the smart guys on the left have known for a long time they are in trouble—and that we are going to dig out their whole structure of programs and power."

According to David Brock, Norquist laid the groundwork for this course of action early on the morning of George W. Bush's inauguration, at a celebratory breakfast of the far right, when he took the podium and declared, "The lefties, the takers, the coercive utopians—they are not stupid, they are evil—EVIL."

In his June 30, 2003, column in *The New York Times*, Paul Krugman points out how Grover Norquist's K Street Project "places Republican activists in high level corporate and industry lobbyists jobs—and excludes Democrats." Rick Santorum, a top-ranking Republican U.S. Senator, and House Majority Leader Tom DeLay and their colleagues have used "intimidation and private threats to bully lobbyists who try to maintain good relations with both parties." This is in tune with Tom DeLay's declaration, "If you want to play in our revolution, you have to live by our rules." Their highly successful enlistment of corporate lobbyists and collection of corporate checks run apace, threateningly moving America toward one-party rule.

The Bush administration's extremely irresponsible financial management has already accomplished its prime objective of starving government for funds. It is also increasingly apparent that the desired result—the downgrading of social programs—is well underway. This goal is the most outrageous and inconsiderate part of the right-wing ideology. It is an attack on the most basic supports relied on by American people: education, health care, housing, food, old-age security and jobs. It is especially demeaning to the needy.

Throughout our nation's history, countless people have benefitted from social services that have enabled them to climb the ladder to a better future. During the 1990s, with the nation's economy prospering and its social service providing major support, much headway was made in helping millions of others to do so. This was especially true within our two largest minority groups, African Americans and Hispanics. They are the groups who will suffer the most from the ongoing imposition of the right-wing's ideology. They have the most to gain by fighting to take back America.

Reacting to the recent jump in unemployment, particularly in low-income neighborhoods, Ciro Rodriguez, chair of the Congressional Hispanic Caucus, said, "As they face a more uncertain future, Hispanics need real solutions not empty promises."

Many African Americans who had moved into higher paying jobs in manufacturing in the 1990s have now lost their jobs and are returning to their old environments. William Lucy, president of the Coalition of Black Trade Unionists, has said, "The number of jobs and the type of jobs that have been lost have severely diminished the standing of many blacks in the middle class." These minorities and others need help from government services, like the help so many of our citizens have received over the years.

It's good to remember, as economists teach us, that every dollar in wages paid to a low income person has many times greater impact in stimulating the economy than one dollar paid to a millionaire. But President Bush gives little attention to such truisms. According to the July 7, 2003, editorial in the Boulder, Colorado, *Daily Camera*, "On social programs, Bush merely talks a good line. But his ultimate intent is never far from the surface of his words. Beneath virtually every administration policy lies a deep-seated commitment to a 50 year-old Republican dream, not just to shrink federal government, but to undo the New Deal."

The Bush administration is well on the way to fulfilling such objectives. Its actions are seriously impacting the cities and states that provide most of our nation's social services in education, health care, food relief, police protection and infrastructure maintenance. They are currently in serious financial difficulty and are cutting deeply into their budgets for such basic services—and destroying jobs in the process.

They need help. The Bush administration should forego some of its tax cuts and use the resulting dollars to immediately provide funds for the states to resume their basic services and keep their employees on the job. But a key goal of Bushites is to cut services. As Thomas Friedman wrote, "Tax cuts are Bushspeak for service cuts." So much for the president's greatly ballyhooed "compassion." What he is really doing is the opposite of compassion; he is abandoning the most needy Americans, encouraging economic inequality and expanding high-poverty neighborhoods, the cradles of violence in America.

The executive director of the National Association of Governors reports that the states have not been in such a sad situation since the Great Depression. States, counties and cities—all are cutting services, laying off people and raising taxes of all kinds. Our most populous state, California, is in the greatest difficulty, with a deficit of over $30 billion. The right-wing Republicans of California, not to be outdone by their national team, went all-out to use their state's financial predicament as a reason for recalling the Democratic governor, Gray Davis. Financed by California Congressman Darrell Issa, they launched their attack just a few months after Davis had been reelected. Their effort to steal the election followed the same pattern as the outrageous attempt by their national colleagues to oust the duly elected President Clinton. The California gang would have been more justified in attacking President Bush. His deficit is much higher on a per capita basis than California's. But, of course, *he doesn't have to balance his budget.*

Our schools also are taking a beating. Colleges, universities and technical schools are being forced to make record increases in tuition. Elementary and high schools are shortening the school year, cutting out or reducing programs, laying off teachers, increasing class size and even terminating maintenance personnel. Even the federal school lunch program, which serves over sixteen million children with free or reduced-price meals, is in trouble. And so are the kids when the school year is over and their free lunches disappear. After-school programs that steer kids away from crime are being dropped. In his budget for 2004 President Bush, obsessed with cutting social programs, called for a 40 percent cut in after-school programs. And Head Start and AmeriCorps, two popular and successful auxiliary education efforts, are being dumped on as well.

On June 26, 2003, following the announcement that New York State Legislature's budget for the coming year included severe education cuts, *New York Times* reporter Bob Herbert wrote:

> There was a time when it was normal for politicians to pay at least some attention to the needs and the longings of middle- and working-class Americans, and the poor. That is how we managed to get (despite conservative opposition) such vital programs as Social Security, Medicare, unemployment insurance, college loans, environmental protections and so forth.
>
> But now the related problems of a tanking economy and the hijacking of federal government assets by the people at the top of the economic pyramid have left little for distressed state and local governments to draw upon for short-term sustenance or long-term recovery. Which is just another way of saying there's very little left for ordinary Americans.
>
> So it's too bad, kids, but this is a new American reality. You'd be getting a windfall if you were one of the high rollers at Bechtel or Halliburton. The game is rigged in their favor. But all you want to do is get a decent education so you can make something of yourself. We can't help you with that.

New York was not the only state where funding for education and social programs had to be slashed, but we have heard nothing from the Bush administration and its extremist colleagues of plans for saving them, for righting this wrong. What an impending tragedy for America!

The stakes are too high for us, the people of the United States, not to blow the whistle.

8

Using Terrorism to Frighten, Threaten and Exploit

The September 11, 2001, terrorist attack on America not only brought down the twin towers of the World Trade Center, a prime symbol of America's economic supremacy, but also severely damaged the Pentagon, the key symbol of America's military preeminence. Three thousand freedom-loving Americans died as a result. It took only fifteen foreigners from the Middle East to accomplish this. They had no weapons of mass destruction, no intercontinental missiles, no aircraft carriers, no fighter planes—just box cutters. With their first-class tickets in hand they safely boarded three of our large domestic airliners (five terrorists to a plane), and when the flights were safely underway, they overpowered the crews, took over the controls and, using these heavily fueled airliners as missiles, headed straight to their targets—and to their own suicides. A fourth plane with four terrorists aboard, apparently aiming for the U.S. Capitol or the White House, failed to reach its target when passengers aboard fought with the terrorists, causing the plane to crash in a field in Pennsylvania.

Watching this catastrophe live on television, Americans, many in tears, were stunned and shaken by this crime against humanity. So was much of the world community, who offered their sympathy and help. President Bush rose to the occasion, promptly visited the sites, offered the nations's sympathy to the bereaved and thanks to the many who pitched in to help the survivors. He vowed to hunt down the leaders of the terrorists, especially their mastermind, Osama bin Laden. Literally overnight, George Bush's stature in America zoomed.

In the days that followed, the broadly diverse people of New York and Washington, D.C., displayed a remarkable unity and resolve as they coped with the devastation they had experienced. People everywhere were amazed by the planning, training, skill, precision and brutality of the terrorists and agreed to work together to combat the world scourge of terrorism. This unity in the face of terror brought a glimmer of hope that something positive might come out of this tragedy for America. But did it?

In his April 15, 2003, speech to the National Press Club, actor Tim Robbins described that hope and how it was extinguished.

> I imagined leadership that would take the incredible energy, this generosity of spirit and create a new unity in America born out of the chaos and tragedy of 9/11, that would send a message to terrorists everywhere: if you attack us, we will become stronger, cleaner, better educated and more unified. You will strengthen our commitment to justice and democracy by your inhumane attacks on us. . . .
>
> And then came the [president's] speech: You are either with us or against us. And the bombing began. And our leader encouraged us to show our patriotism by shopping and by volunteering to join groups that would turn in their neighbor for any suspicious behavior.
>
> In the 19 months since 9/11, we have seen our democracy compromised by fear and hatred. Basic inalienable rights, due process, the sanctity of the home have been quickly compromised in a climate of fear. A unified American public has grown bitterly divided, and a world population that had found profound sympathy and support for us has grown contemptuous and distrustful.

How did this come about? President Bush, Karl Rove, Vice President Cheney and others around them, sensing the power and sudden increased popularity of the commander in chief engendered by 9/11, decided to capitalize on it to advance their radical agenda. Fanning the fear, talking tough and waving the sword became prime activities. Out of this came the Department of Homeland Security and its color-coded terror index. Four times in one year the department ratchetted the code up from yellow (elevated) to orange (high risk) when some unspecified, but imminent, threat was presumed. Each time millions of Americans cowered, their duct tape at the ready, their refrigerators well stocked. The higher the code, the higher the fear. How different this administration's demagogic reaction was from President Franklin D. Roosevelt's to the economic and world problems of his first administration: "We have nothing to fear but fear itself."

As *Newsweek* reported on June 2, 2003, "Americans could not be blamed for weariness, doubt, and a touch of cynicism. Is Code Orange little more than a bureaucratic device that allows nervous policymakers to cover themselves, just in case something does go wrong? Could it be that the Bush administration wants to remind voters from time to time that the terrorists are still out there—and that it takes a strong commander in chief to stand tall against the threat?"

Paul Campos, a law professor at the University of Colorado, stated on May 29, 2003, "The war on terrorism is a good deal more frightening than terrorism itself, because the measures taken in its name are likely to pose a far greater danger to the average American than Osama bin Laden or any of his miserable imitators. . . . If our government took the same attitude toward auto fatalities that it takes toward terrorism, driving would be illegal."

The risk to any of us 270 million Americans from a terrorist attack, even one as serious as 9/11, is very low—much lower than the risks involved in smoking tobacco, drinking alcohol, dying in a fire at home, being locked up, owning a handgun, serving in the armed forces, being raped or murdered or dying in a violent storm. What if another terrorist attack in America killed four thousand people? Would we be better protected by living in a state of fear ahead of time? Or by knowing that over 99.998 percent of us would escape?

Two days after 9/11 President Bush said, "The most important thing is for us to find Osama bin Laden. It is our number one priority and we will not rest until we find him." Six months later the president admitted, "I don't know where bin Laden is. I have no idea and really don't care. It's not that important." Ten months later, in his January 2003 State of the Union address, he mentioned al Qaeda but said not a word about their elusive leader. By then the president's attention had shifted to another bogeyman, Saddam Hussein, who, he claimed, had weapons of mass destruction, constituted an imminent threat to America and was in bed with Osama bin Laden and his terrorists. Now we know that all three of those claims were false.

Currently the president appears to have forgotten bin Laden altogether. Instead he is focused on hunting down Saddam Hussein and killing what he calls the terrorists within Iraq. As a consequence, we are hated in the Middle East more than ever before. Worse yet, the relationship between the United States and these terrorists is markedly changed. Because we invaded and occupied their land, they find it easy, even inviting, to attack Americans. They don't have to travel seven thousand miles from home to do so. Moreover, sympathizers from neighboring middle-eastern countries are streaming across the borders to help their Iraqi brothers sabotage American efforts to restore peace and stability. Right there on familiar soil they find convenient targets in the form of 150,000 members of our armed services and thousands of others sent there to help with the restoration and rehabilitation of Iraq.

What began as a difficult circumstance for our troops has been made all the more so by the Bush administration's decision to act unilaterally rather than working with the UN to get rid of Saddam Hussein. How much better it would have been if the United Nations had been allowed to bring its worldwide force and authority to bear in ousting the Iraqi dictator.

Here at home our American way of life is threatened by the Bush administration's trying to ride the wave of national patriotism to gain sweeping changes. The Pentagon uses the threat to push legislation through Congress to exempt the military from major environmental laws. Vice President Cheney and Secretary Rumsfeld use it in an effort to justify their high-priority project to bring about, through unilateral military power, a Pax Americana—a peaceful world dominated by the United States. As Deborah Stapelkamp wrote in the July 13, 2003, issue of the *Unitarian Bulletin*, "Our government tells us the terrorists resent our American freedom and then cloaks its violations of our Bill of Rights and our Constitution in the flag of patriotism and righteousness, and cows us into accepting the loss of our freedoms, by instilling in us the fear that our homeland will not be safe otherwise."

That is a good description of the performance of John Ashcroft, attorney general of the United States of America and head of our Department of Justice. Our American way of life is not safe with him in that vital position, for he is at the heart of the vast right-wing conspiracy.

According to former insider David Brock, when Ashcroft was to appear before the Senate for confirmation, his defense in that bitter battle was planned in strategy sessions of the far-right movement presided over by the czar of the movement, Grover Norquist. Brock writes that Ashcroft was among the shrillest voices for the impeachment of President Clinton, an act orchestrated by that movement. He is a close ally of Pat Robertson and other Christian rightists who do not share America's devotion to separation of church and state. Worse yet, he fits no one's notions of unity or inclusiveness and even has ties to a neo-Confederate magazine, writes Brock.

In Brock's words, "Ashcroft was sworn in by Clarence Thomas, who paid back the conservative allies to whom he was beholden. . . . Thomas, who gave the Francis Boyer Lecture at the American Enterprise Institute's conservative prom just after the inauguration in early 2001, denigrated the importance of civility and moderation in politics, bemoaned the 'culture of death' code phrase for abortion rights and euthanasia, and lustily observed that the country was in the midst of 'not a civil war but a culture war.'"

How can a justice of our Supreme Court say such things?

Such a man as Ashcroft *can* be judged by the company he keeps. He named Ted Olson to be solicitor general of the United States and Larry Thompson to be deputy attorney general. Both are stalwart and longtime members of the far-right conveniently placed in the two top positions under Ashcroft. Ted Olson, Kenneth Starr's best friend, according to Brock, has been a board member of the *American Spectator*, the right-wing conspiracy's prime publication. They were only a few denizens of the far-right who joined George W. Bush's team. As David Brock puts it, "As Bush's government was assembled, with Clarence Thomas's wife Ginni handling the flow of resumes from the Heritage Foundation over to the White House personnel office, many of the key players made up a rogue's gallery from my past."

Then, just forty-five days after 9/11, Congress passed a sweeping anti-terrorism bill crafted by Attorney General Ashcroft. It gave his Department of Justice extraordinary powers to investigate, apprehend, lock up and detain any person suspected of supporting terrorism. The bill was called The U.S.A. Patriot Act, another example of Bushspeak, of his administration's penchant for naming activities something they are not.

Immediately the Justice Department adopted a series of draconian measures to exert its new powers, some of which clearly violated the U.S. Bill of Rights. Here is part of the ACLU's response: "Did you know that it is now legal for government agents to break into your home when you are away, conduct a search—and keep you from finding out for days, weeks or even months that a warrant was ever issued? That they can get the courts to rubber stamp their demands for information about the books you read. . . . [and even] obtain your credit reports and other sensitive information without judicial approval and without your consent?"

Promptly, civil liberties groups nationwide condemned their actions and challenged their legality through the American Civil Liberties Union (ACLU), arguing that "The U.S.A. Patriot Act went far beyond fighting terrorism—removing the checks and balances that have helped prevent police and other law enforcement agents from abusing their power. It allowed government agents to violate our civil liberties—tapping deep into the private lives of innocent Americans."

By July 30, 2003, after months of debate around the country, the ACLU and six Muslim groups sued Attorney General Ashcroft, challenging the constitutionality of the Act. The Justice Department claimed the Act was needed "to protect our citizens from savage attacks such as those which occurred on September 11, 2001."

Anthony Lewis provided a good example of what our Department of Justice now considers justifiable. He wrote in *The New York Times Magazine* on April 20, 2003:

> Forty years ago, the Supreme Court found that the Constitution guaranteed the right to a lawyer. Maybe the Bush administration hasn't read the decision.
>
> In two cases now before the courts, Attorney General John Ashcroft is asserting that President Bush has the power to detain any American citizen indefinitely, in solitary confinement, without access to a lawyer, if he, the president, designates the detainee an "enemy combatant." The detainee cannot effectively challenge that designation. . . .
>
> I would not have believed that an attorney general would argue that an American could be held indefinitely without being able to speak to a lawyer. I seriously doubt that any attorney general in the past 40 years since Gideon [the Supreme Court decision], except the present occupant of that office, would have made that claim.

Lewis cites the present case of Jose Papilla, a Muslim who had previously served time in prison and who was arrested by federal agents on

May 8, 2002. A judge appointed a competent lawyer to represent him at a federal grand jury hearing scheduled for June 11, 2002. But on June 10, Ashcroft, who happened to be in Moscow, made a televised statement accusing Papilla of being a terrorist. Papilla never got to the grand jury.

Lewis described how Papilla is now locked up in a Navy brig in South Carolina. Neither his court-appointed lawyer nor a federal judge who wanted to examine the evidence for claiming Papilla an "enemy combatant" has been allowed to see him. A government affidavit claimed that "any access to counsel, however brief, can undo months of work and may permanently shut down the interrogation process." Of this, Lewis wrote, "The very fact that extended interrogation in the absence of counsel may break a subject's will is one reason that the right to counsel is guaranteed in criminal law." The Department of Justice claims that allowing counsel would interfere with the interrogation process.

Ralph G. Ness, president of People for the American Way, in a recent letter to members, described "the shameful realities that have accompanied the government's war on terrorism here at home. The post-9/11 civil rights abuses are nearing the end of their second year, and they are growing more alarming—and more dangerous—to the precious traditions of liberty that have been fought for over 225 years." He points out that after "the Justice Department's own inspector general documented appalling violations of the civil and constitutional rights of 9/11 detainees, John Ashcroft's office responded incredibly 'We make no apologies.' "

Mr. Attorney General, have you no shame? You are attacking our most basic constitutional rights and taking us back to the days of Joseph McCarthy. While keeping your own activities secret, you pry into the innermost lives of individual citizens.

The human rights group, Amnesty International, released its annual report on May 28, 2003. Sarah Lyall, reporting on the event in *The New York Times*, noted that "The world has become more dangerous and governments more repressive, since the effort to fight terrorism began after the September 11, 2001, attacks on the United States. . . . " She also states that "The group singled out the United States for particular opprobrium, condemning its detention of 600 foreign nationals at Guantanamo Bay, Cuba, as a 'human rights scandal' and calling on the government to release or charge those held there."

Lyall also quotes Irene Khan, Amnesty's secretary general as saying: "What would have been unacceptable on Sept. 10, 2001, is now becoming almost the norm," and that "far from making the world a safer place, has made it more dangerous by curtailing human rights, undermining the rule of international law, and shielding governments from scrutiny."

In reaction to the increasing flood of criticism to his Patriot Act, Attorney General John Ashcroft set out on a national tour on August 19, 2003. His plan was to defend the Act by speaking to private groups—mainly law enforcement groups, not public gatherings. As one might expect, his first stop was at a safe port, the American Enterprise Institute, the prime gathering ground and launching platform for the far-right extremists. There he claimed "any attempt to strip law enforcement agents of their expanded [after 9/11] legal powers could open the way to further terrorist attacks. To abandon these tools would senselessly imperil American lives and American liberty, and it would ignore the lessons of September 11." He then argued that the Patriot Act had saved America from additional terrorist attacks—but he failed to identify any of them.

The Ashcroft tour was supposed to pave the way for his Domestic Security Enhancement Act of 2003 (Patriot Act II), which would markedly increase the government's power to subvert or ignore our basic human rights, even going so far as to suspend the writ of habeas corpus. Even William Safire, the conservative columnist, calls this "an abomination" and Congressman Jerold Nadler says it is "little more than the institution of a police state."

Yet Attorney General Ashcroft shows no sign of relenting or rethinking. His current activities, like those of the president and other members of his team, are increasingly pointed toward the 2004 reelection campaign and keeping 9/11 front and center. Adam Nagourney and Philip Shenon wrote about this in the July 31, 2003, issue of *The New York Times*, "To what extent is it appropriate for the imagery of 9/11 to be incorporated into the political appeals of Mr. Bush and his Democratic opponent? Is there a risk that voters will recoil at a perception that a candidate is stage-managing tragedy for political gain, particularly with each side already accusing the other of doing just that?"

I am confident that American voters will sort this out appropriately. But to do so they will first have to cope with and decipher the growing barrage of attacks the Bush administration makes on its critics by questioning their patriotism. The frightening effectiveness of this Karl Rove tactic was displayed in the 2002 congressional elections when it was used to defeat three Democratic Senators running for reelection—Max Cleland (Georgia), Jean Carnahan (Missouri) and Jean Shaheen (New Hampshire). That this tactic was extremely *unpatriotic* was especially documented in the defeat of Max Cleland, the celebrated veteran who had lost three limbs in the Vietnam War.

Russell Hemenway, national director of the venerable and respected National Committee for an Effective Congress, took off his nonpartisan gloves in a letter dated August 14, 2003, writing "Despite the fact that all [these] candidates were strong supporters of homeland security legislation, they were subjected to a drumbeat of questioning about their patriotism and, right up to the closing of the polls, they were relentlessly charged with being 'soft on terrorism.'"

Hemenway also described how the same pattern of demagoguery was now being used to attack Democrats in general after Senator Richard Durbin (D, Illinois), a member of the Senate Select Intelligence Committee, revealed that CIA Director Tenet had named the White House official who had insisted that the false uranium claim be included in the president's State of the Union address. "This was on July 16, (2003)," wrote Hemenway. "Every day since then Republicans have relentlessly charged that Democrats, in their zeal to score political points, have sacrificed the national interest on the altar of partisan politics and are making accusations which are offensive against the president."

Earlier I described Grover Norquist's key role in the leadership of the Republican right-wing extremists and Karl Rove's primacy in the Bush hierarchy. Here is what Hemenway wrote about them:

> Norquist and Karl Rove, both raised in Texas politics, are as thick as thieves. It's often difficult to discern which one is the ventriloquist and who is the talking dog. Over the coming months it is they who will be writing the script and choreographing the 2004 elections. Both are skilled in the use of the big lie technique which entails distortion, disparagement and unrelenting repetition.
>
> This is gutter politics at its worst.
>
> They have also played a key role in creating a climate in America where those who disagree with their government are labeled

unpatriotic, disloyal or even traitors. It is good to recall what Republican President Theodore Roosevelt said about criticism of the president. "To announce that there must be no criticism of the president, or that we are to stand by the president right or wrong, is not only unpatriotic and servile, but is morally treasonable to the American public.

With that in mind, it's worth recalling some of the questionable statements made by our current national leaders.

Responding to questions concerning what the president knew prior to 9/11 about possible terrorist attacks, Vice President Cheney in May 2002 said: "[Democrats] need to be very cautious not to seek political advantage by making incendiary suggestions. . . . Such commentary is thoroughly irresponsible and totally unworthy of national leaders in a time of war."

Concerned about criticism of the president's reasons for wanting to go to war with Iraq, Ari Fleischer, White House press secretary, warned at a press briefing on September 26, 2002, "These are reminders to all Americans that they need to watch what they say, watch what they do, and this is not a time for remarks like that. There never is."

And from Attorney General Ashcroft on December 6, 2001: "To those who scare peace-loving people with phantoms of lost liberty, my message is this: Your tactics only aid terrorists for they erode our national unity and diminish our resolve. They give ammunition to America's enemies."

Speaker of the House Dennis Hastert (March 18, 2002): "Those comments may not undermine the president as he leads us into war, and they may not give comfort to our adversaries, but they come mighty close,"

And finally, House Majority Leader Tom DeLay on March 20, 2003, "This destructive rhetoric does nothing more than demoralize our troops and second-guess our commander in chief."

Today the fallout from such leadership has grown frighteningly to the point where prominent entertainers, reporters, columnists, TV hosts and speakers are being hounded publicly—reprimanded, booed and some even fired—for criticizing the president.

So you see, fellow Americans, we are engaged in a war of words. My advice is to be honest, to promptly challenge those who try to scare us off and to stand up for what we know to be right. If we don't, our friends, relatives and descendants might well find us guilty of complicity in this culture of fear and repression.

9

A Call to Action

Fellow Patriots, Stand Up!

Stand up to honor the great nation we have inherited and the many generations who have built it.

Stand up for our American way of life with its freedoms, justice under law, enviable standard of living and opportunity to choose our own leaders.

Stand up for the heroes who have led America, fought for her, died for her, conquered her enemies from within and without—colonization, slavery, Fascism and Communism—and won the respect and admiration of the peoples of the world.

Stand up for the basic foundations of our way of life—the Declaration of Independence, the Constitution with its Bill of Rights and the Charter of the United Nations.

And listen as well, for America is crying for us to save her hard-earned way of life—to save it from her current extremist leaders who, as I have shown in the previous eight chapters, are rapidly propelling us down a foreboding and alien path, using any means to reach their own personal goals, selling out the baby boomers and their children and bullying our people with continuous warnings of impending terrorist attacks.

On their side is the most powerful office in the world, the presidency of the United States of America, the most powerful war machine in history and many of our nation's wealthiest individuals, including some potent captains of industry.

On our side, there is an even more powerful force, the ballot. We must use it wisely to save our American way of life, one that:
•honors integrity
•protects our basic human rights
•fosters life, liberty and the pursuit of happiness for every American
•safeguards democracy from evil
•furthers the opportunity for everyone to climb the ladder to a better tomorrow
•supports freedom of enterprise
•furthers health care for all
•safeguards social security
•insures a quality education for everyone
•works through the United Nations to resolve international problems and pursue world peace
•protects local and global environmental quality
•fights fiscal irresponsibility
•supports a strong modern military that is kept out of the clutches of the military-industrial complex, as President Eisenhower advised us

We don't need to transform America, as the Bush administration is doing. We need to return to the-well proven path of our American way of life, solve our current problems and provide for the future. It is our solemn duty to take back America. We patriots can can do that if we stand up, stand together and put our democracy to work. Now is the time to give patriotism its true meaning.